CW00926798

THE ART OF THE AUTOMOBILE

THE DEFINITIVE HISTORY OF THE FINEST CARS EVER MADE

Zef Enault

Nicolas Heidet

PREFACE

Anthony Beltoise

MITCHELL
BEAZLEY

PREFACE

People have never been indifferent to the Jaguar marque, either for its air of prestige or its performances on the track. Few manufacturers can boast that they have combined luxury, elegance and performance so effectively in their cars. The personality of Jaguar's founder Sir William Lyons – at once cold and phlegmatic, fiery and irascible – could not leave me indifferent either. The story of the company reflects his temperament, wholly contradictory yet with a single goal: the triumph of his marque.

The victories of the C-type and D-type in the Le Mans 24 Hours left their mark on the pantheon of endurance racing. And the marque's stunning return to Le Mans in the 1980s and 1990s, with its XJRs, continued this wonderful story. Jaguar has always known how to evolve and take risks. The marque's arrival in Formula One with the R1 in 2000 proved this, even though the car's engine came from Ford. The marque's emblem and its credibility were at stake: it took a lot of courage to take on such seasoned competition. The electric Formula E cars were born of the same recklessness, a perpetual desire to forge ahead. Several companies have taken possession of the British marque during the course of its history, but none has ever been able (or perhaps willing) to alter its strong identity.

> "How many crowned heads have ridden in a Jaguar at the same time as the British marque was competing fiercely in a motor race?"

This is rooted above all in certain legendary models, from the XK120 to the E-type – not forgetting the great XJ6. How many crowned heads have ridden in a Jaguar at the same time as the British marque was competing fiercely in a motor race, be that a rally, endurance race or speed event? What car collector has never dreamed of possessing an XKSS or an E-type Lightweight, while using an F-type for their day-to-day driving?

Over the years, Jaguar has been able to adapt to the car market without in any way betraying its DNA. Obviously, the first diesel engines, like the first SUV, risked getting a poor reception, but the marque's strength lies in its capacity to renew itself without losing any of its identity. This is why I am proud to represent it today, racing in Monaco at the wheel of the I-Pace eTrophy. Jaguar is a marque unlike any other!

Anthony Beltoise
Winner of the 1992 Volant Elf, second at the 2000 Le Mans 24 Hours, winner of the 2005 Carrera Cup, champion of the French FFSA GT in 2011 and 2012. Jaguar ambassador. Son of the Formula One racing driver Jean-Pierre Beltoise.

RIGHT
William Lyons was interested in the export of cars from the start. These 1946 Jaguar Mark IV saloons are ready to embark for the United States.

BELOW LEFT
The young William Lyons was passionate about motorbikes. Here he is on his Harley-Davidson in 1920.

BELOW RIGHT
William Lyons, alongside an E-Type from 1961. He said: "The car is the closest thing we will ever create to something that is alive."

FOREWORD

If the name of William Lyons has remained forever linked to the Jaguar marque – rather than that of William Walmsley, who co-founded the SS company (later Jaguar) with him – it is because of his courage tinged with dishonesty, not to mention his penny-pinching. When the two young men were still manufacturing Swallow sidecars, Lyons met the famous George Brough, father of the Brough Superior, the "Rolls Royce of motorcycles". Lyons borrowed a Brough Superior to use in an exhibition of Swallow sidecars at the London Motor Show, on a stand that was not even his. A few decades later, he had no qualms sending a telegram to Queen Elizabeth II on the day of her coronation in 1953, dedicating to her the victory of the Jaguar C-type in the Le Mans 24 Hours. He was knighted three years later.

Another anecdote details the way in which Lyons silenced an American customer who told him at a show that the heating in his XK140 was not working. Lyons started the engine, turned on the heating and held a cigarette in front of the vents. The smoke was blown back slightly. He cried: "Your heating is working," to which the customer replied that it was -15°C (5°F). Lyons retorted: "Just put on a coat!"

We could have written this book about Jaguar by simply telling more of these little stories, as Sir William's career was full of them, but we didn't. We could have described all the Jaguar models, but we chose to leave some out. It was all down to choice. Instead, we have endeavoured to relate the richness of the Jaguar story through its cars (some of them legendary, others less so), through a chronology of events, as well as Jaguar's exploits in competition. Photographs play a crucial role in this task. They illustrate the development of Jaguar, where tradition and modernity have always gone hand in hand.

We hope that this book will meet the expectations of readers new to the story of this important British marque.

The authors,
Zef Enault and Nicolas Heidet

CONTENTS

Chapter 1

H I S T O R Y

From three wheels to four

1922 › 1945

Swallow, the small company founded by the young William Walmsley at the start of the 20th century, quickly became the foundation of a firm friendship with William Lyons, and it was from here that the great Jaguar story sprang. This was a time of daring pioneers, who, often working from a small lean-to or, better still, a tiny brick garage, won fame in many areas: bicycles, planes, cars, motorbikes and more. The world was their oyster, and England was crawling with adventurers getting their hands dirty, passionate about the development of their (sometimes disconcerting) contraptions. Among these enthusiasts were the founder of Triumph, Siegfried Bettmann, and, on the other side of the Atlantic, William Harley and Arthur Davidson, the creators of Harley-Davidson. The way that Walmsley and Lyons met, incidentally, bears odd similarities to the meeting of those Americans.

Born in 1892 in Stockport, England, Walmsley went to work in his father's small coal business early on. Like many young men at the time, he enlisted in the army to fight in World War One, where he developed a strong interest in motorcycles that stayed with him after the war was over. Motorcycles were then very much in fashion – cars were more expensive and the preserve of the wealthy – and many Europeans travelled by motorcycle. Lacking funds, Walmsley quickly became involved in

working with the machinery, having learned the basics at his father's company. Starting with a Triumph frame, he built his own motorbike.

But the young Walmsley was not only passionate about machinery – he was interested in women, too. As comfort for two passengers was not a feature of motorcycles during the 1910s (and at a time when sidecars were just wicker baskets), he embarked on the construction of an octagonal, aluminium sidecar. By an ironic twist of fate, Harley-Davidson did the same, a few months before Walmsley. And, as with Harley and Davidson, a house move led to Walmsley meeting Lyons, which would produce another famous duo.

One swallow made a summer

When Walmsley's family moved to Blackpool in 1921, the young sidecar builder went with them. They settled in the same neighbourhood as a young man named William Lyons, whose father owned a shop selling musical instruments. Walmsley quickly became intrigued by these curious devices. Lyons himself had been sent by his father to work as an apprentice at an automobile manufacturer, Crossley Motors. He loved motorcycles, and had bought a few. It seems that Walmsley and Lyons were destined to meet – Lyons purchased a sidecar from Walmsley, and the two men struck up a friendship.

The first Swallow Sidecar Company plant, in Blackpool, during a period of prosperity.

In an era when most sidecars were octagonal, Swallow sidecars stood out among competitors due to their modern and original design.

The Swallow Sidecar Company's stand at the London Motor Show in 1922. William Lyons was quick to grasp the importance of good communication in business.

William Walmsley, at the wheel, and his associate, William Lyons, in the sidecar. This was the beginning of a great adventure, although the former would soon abandon ship.

It took Lyons some time to persuade his new friend to let him become involved in his business, but perseverance was already one of Lyons' established personality traits. The sidecar business, now officially named Swallow, then began to get more serious. The two Williams, helped by their parents, had invested a small amount of capital and found small, brick-built premises in which to manufacture the Swallow sidecar. The model's superb design quickly earned it many customers. It was soon necessary to acquire bigger premises, hire staff and even deal with a few export orders. Over the years, the Swallow Sidecar Company's range was expanded.

Meanwhile, the motorcar was developing rapidly and threatening to put sidecars in the shade. Lyons, who had worked in the car sector, sensed that the company needed to progress. In 1926, he bought a chassis from the British car manufacturer Austin, with the intention of fitting it with more elegant Swallow bodywork. The Austin Seven was born. In 1927 it was developed, and began to sell well.

In 1928, despite some disagreement over Lyons' eagerness, Lyons and Walmsley decided to pursue their car adventure. They launched the Austin Swallow Saloon, styled by Cyril Holland, a designer they had hired to work on sidecars. The Saloon was a little more luxurious and comfortable than the Seven, but still affordable. Production was constantly being increased and it became necessary to find bigger premises again, this time in the city of Coventry, in England's industrial heartland. The company then hired some 50 people, of whom 32 followed it to Coventry. Holland was not among these, preferring to stay in Blackpool.

Stock market flotation

The Austin Swallow models were developed during the 1920s and 1930s. They came in various versions, such as the Standard Swallow and Standard Nine. Other models used a chassis made by Fiat or a platform by Wolseley – such as the sporty 1931 Wolseley Swallow, which had a six-cylinder engine. It was not until this stage that the two Williams had the idea to develop their own chassis and then, later, their own engines. They joined forces with a manufacturer: Standard Motor Company. This agreement gave birth to the SS (Standard Swallow) One, the first car from this new brand, launched in October 1931 at the London Motor Show. However, the engine's modest power output of 45bhp was not enough for Lyons and, in 1933, the SS1 was fitted with a more powerful six-cylinder engine. The car began to be entered in competitions to promote the new brand, SS Cars Ltd, founded in the same year. At the time, rallies were very popular, and in competition the SS cars demonstrated their qualities. The company even hired a press officer, Ernest Rankin. It succeeded in overcoming the difficulties of the 1930s economic crisis, thanks to the SS models' attractive prices. For a long time, Jaguar cars would stand out for the same reason.

The relationship between Walmsley and Lyons progressively deteriorated as their business developed. Walmsley was less passionate and rigorous about his work and ended up selling his stake to Lyons during the winter of 1934. The money he made he invested in a small business that made trailers and, later, caravans, and he was finally able to devote himself to his favourite hobby: model railways.

From then on, Lyons took decisions alone, even though he was not the sole member of the board of SS Cars Ltd, which floated on the stock market in 1935. He was determined to increase the power of his cars, and had Standard engines prepared for this purpose. To do this, he called on the services of the famous engineer Harry Weslake, a specialist in internal combustion engines. Their association would not end there.

1929

The Fiat Swallow, the Standard Swallow... Walmsley and Lyons were firing on all cylinders.

Swallow's automobile assembly line in 1929 – proving that building a car is no easy task.

In 1928, the Swallow business was determined to improve the appearance of Morris Cowley cars (the open car version is shown here), with a new and lowered body.

Once assembled, the little Austin Swallows were displayed at the Blackpool plant.

Austin
Seven Swallow
1927

An aesthete

Although the motorcycle and sidecar turned out to be the most popular means of motorized transport during the 1910s, thanks to their low cost, in the following decade the motorcar gradually became more accessible – notably the Ford Model T in the United States and the Austin Seven in Britain. The Austin marque, founded by Sir Herbert Austin, caught the eye of the young William Lyons and his associate William Walmsley, who felt that the market for motorcars looked promising. But the sidecars they manufactured under the Swallow name risked suffering as a result, especially as they had just hired the talented coachbuilder Cyril Holland. Lyons went in search of an Austin Seven in order to fit it with bodywork that was to his taste – a common practice at the time. In January 1927, he persuaded the Austin dealer in Bolton, Lancashire, to sell him a bare chassis for £114. Lyons, Walmsley and Holland set to work.

Using the Austin's ash frame as a base, they came up with a body that was more elegant than the original. Their skill in shaping aluminium sheets, acquired through the manufacture of sidecars, as well as the good taste of Lyons and Holland, enabled them to create the Austin Seven Swallow quickly. By the spring of 1927, the first Swallow car was ready. The seats were leather-covered, and the instruments were set in a dashboard of polished mahogany. The little convertible was also available with either a soft top or a removable rigid roof. The 747cc engine was retained, unchanged. The figure of a swallow crested the radiator. A few orders came in quickly, followed by a larger one at the end of the year – for 50 cars from a dealer in Birmingham. Over five years, 3,500 Swallows were made.

OPPOSITE
This 1927 Swallow Sport two-seater was released at the same time as the first advertisements.

Austin Seven Swallow, 1927

DISPLACEMENT: inline four-cylinder, 747cc; **MAX POWER:** 10.5bhp; **TORQUE:** unknown; naturally aspirated; rear-wheel drive; three-speed manual gearbox; **WEIGHT:** 390kg (860lb).

SS One
SS Two

1931

A foot on the ladder

Competition in the market for attractive, reasonably priced cars - still a very niche market at the time - intensified at the start of the 1930s. William Lyons felt, more than his associate William Walmsley, deeply committed to the sector and put his heart and soul into it. While continuing to build sidecars, the Swallow Company became increasingly involved in motorcars. Having used Austin, Fiat and Wolseley chassis, it became obvious to Lyons that they needed to develop their own chassis, even if they lacked the ability to build their own engines.

Swallow made an agreement with Standard to produce the first SS model, its initials - according to legend, but never confirmed or denied by Lyons - standing for the initials of the two companies. Lyons, incidentally, got on well with Standard's boss, John Black.

The fashion at the time was for cars with a low roof, and the design of the SS1 followed suit. However, before its launch in the summer of 1931, while Lyons was in hospital, Walmsley had the roof raised, fearing the design had gone too far. On his return to work, Lyons flew

into a rage, before admitting that perhaps Walmsley was right…

The SS1 created a sensation when it was unveiled at the 1931 London Motor Show. The first road tests reported in the press confirmed first impressions. The SS1's elegance caused a stir, all the more because its price was modest. Its rivals lacked such a sumptuous appearance. However, its six-cylinder, 2-litre engine, which produced 45bhp, did not endow it with the sort of performance its appearance suggested. Some road testers in the specialist press did not fail to point this out.

Lyons developed a new version of the SS1 in 1932, featuring a new Standard chassis. Later, Swallow fitted a new Standard engine that was more powerful (by some 20bhp), thanks to a displacement of 2.5 litres. The SS1 was subsequently offered in a range of different versions, starting with a four-seater Tourer, unveiled in March 1933. A saloon (sedan) and two coupés followed.

At the time, the richest customers gravitated towards Bentley and other prestigious marques, but many coachbuilders would take production models and modify their appearance to tempt the new, well-

OPPOSITE
This superb 1932 SS Coupé One Helmet Wing already exemplified the elegance of future Jaguars.

ABOVE
These SS1s were the first to be shipped to the United States. The year was 1934.

RIGHT
Manufactured between 1931 and 1935, the SS1 Tourer measured 15¾ft (4.8m) long.

off clientele. SS quickly became a brand that was well known for transforming Standard models.

SS cars were soon entered into competitions, initially in England, and then in more prestigious races such as the Coupe des Alpes in France, achieving a number of wins.

From 1931, another model was available alongside the SS1: the SS2, with a chassis derived from a Standard frame and a four-cylinder engine producing just 27bhp. In 1934, two other engines, also four-cylinder, allowed the model to achieve more appealing power outputs: a 1,343cc engine producing 32bhp and a 1,608cc engine producing 38bhp. The SS2 was available both as a coupé and as a saloon.

In 1935, the SS range was further broadened by a sports version, the SS 90. It featured the 2.5-litre engine of the SS1, set in a shortened SS1 chassis, with a wheelbase reduced to that of the SS2. It was named 90 because it was supposed to be able to reach 90mph. Its engine had been set up to offer more power than the SS1, thanks to a higher compression ratio, an aluminium cylinder head and special connecting rods. It was the first sporty "Jaguar" – but the SS 100 then eclipsed it totally.

SS One/SS Two

Although not as prestigious as the Bentley, the SS soon found its audience.

Jaguar SS One, 1931 — **DISPLACEMENT:** inline six-cylinder, 2,054cc; **MAX POWER:** 45bhp; **TORQUE:** unknown; naturally aspirated; rear-wheel drive; four-speed manual gearbox; **WEIGHT:** 1,100kg (2,425lb).

SS 100
1935

Beauty

OPPOSITE
The SS 100 differed
from the SS 90 in the
rear, which was a little
less abrupt, and by
the design of its front
wings (fenders). But its
mechanics were what
ultimately set it apart
from its predecessors.

William Lyons sensed that, with the rise of Nazism in Germany, it would be necessary to come up with another name for his cars. He wanted to use "Sunbeam", but this had already been taken up by another brand. On the other hand, SS evoked the finest British motorcycles of the time, the Brough Superiors, and had a sporting connotation that Lyons always liked. Sadly, history would deal a fatal blow to the double "S".

Nevertheless, new SS cars were launched in 1935 in the footsteps of the SS1 and SS2 and, for the first time, the saloons were given the name Jaguar as well as the letters SS. The SS Jaguar 2.5-litre Saloon, featuring a six-cylinder engine, was unveiled with great fanfare in London. The SS Jaguar 1.5-litre, with a four-cylinder engine, featured alongside it.

The sporty SS 100 (although from 1936 it would be known as the SS Jaguar 100) did not cause as much of a stir at its launch but, nevertheless, made its mark in the history of the motorcar. The SS 100 followed the SS 90, which it resembled quite closely in terms of look, although its rear was modified. It had a top speed of 100mph, thanks to its 2.6-litre six-cylinder engine, whose top end had been redesigned by the engineers William Heynes and Harry Weslake. A new cylinder head with overhead valves replaced the previous sidevalve arrangement; this, along with freer-flowing inlet and exhaust manifolds, greatly improved the intake of the fuel mixture and the expulsion of exhaust gases.

It wasn't long before the SS 100 entered competitions, notably the Coupe Internationale des Alpes in 1936, a rally organized by the Automobile Club de France, where it had a surprising win in a special stage, beating a Bugatti. In 1937 and 1938, Jack Harrop drove the SS 100 to victory in the famous RAC Rally in Britain, which was very popular with the public. These sporting achievements, together with its flowing lines, increased the car's popularity.

Three years after its launch, the SS 100 was given a new, reworked engine based on the previous six-cylinder unit, with a displacement of 3.5 litres, and a new four-speed gearbox (transmission). Power was increased to 125bhp at 4,500 rpm, and the top

ABOVE
This 1937 SS Jaguar 100 is still in use today. In 2011 it competed in Austria's Südsteiermark Classic Rally. Few owners would risk putting such a jewel on the road.

RIGHT
The first SS 100 2.7-litre engine was created by Standard and then modified by the engineers Harry Weslake and William Heynes.

speed went up by 6mph to a claimed 106mph. The British magazine *Autocar* clocked it at 101mph, meaning the SS figure was not far off the mark.

Today, SS 100 cars are sought-after because so few were made: 198 with the 2.6-litre engine, and just 116 with the later 3.5-litre six-cylinder engine. Manufacturing, especially of high-end cars, was nothing like it is today. Cars were expensive during the 1930s, and most people travelled by bicycle or small-engine motorcycle. At the time, the SS Jaguar 100 was comparable to a BMW 328 or a Bugatti Type 57, which meant that it was one of the most prestigious cars of the interwar years.

Some replicas were built during the 1980s, using the XK 4.2-litre engine (Birchfield Sports) or the 3.4-litre and 4.2-litres engines from the XJ6 (Suffolk SS100).

SS 100
Only 116 cars were ever given a 3.5-litre engine.

Jaguar SS 100, 1935

DISPLACEMENT: inline six-cylinder, 2,663cc; **MAX POWER:** 102bhp; **TORQUE:** 133lb ft; naturally aspirated; rear-wheel drive; four-speed manual gearbox; **WEIGHT:** 1,100kg (2,425lb).

HISTORY

Successes and setbacks

1945 › 1961

Like the rest of British industry, SS was obliged to take part in the war effort during World War Two. The longer the war went on, the more the company was forced to scale down its normal operations in the field of motorcars and sidecars. But production of the SS 100 and other 2½ Saloons continued despite everything, with engines being adapted to run on lower-quality petrol (gas).

From 1935, William Lyons used the name Jaguar to designate the Saloon model. He balked at applying the initials SS to this prestigious car, and so a list of names was drawn up. The list comprised numerous words for animals, including Jaguar. The big cat was chosen because of what it symbolized: grace and power. SS then began, during the 1930s and 1940s, to add Jaguar to its usual initials, and in 1937, the company Jaguar Cars Ltd was formed as a subsidiary of SS Cars Ltd. After the end of the war in 1945, the letters SS were dropped for obvious reasons. Only the Jaguar name was retained.

The war had not affected Jaguar's production facility too badly, but obtaining supplies of raw materials became difficult, and rationing was in place. In 1948, Lyons decided to relinquish the manufacture of sidecars, and sold off the Swallow brand. In the meantime, Jaguar cars were once again made available to dealers, with no modifications other than a few cost-saving measures as regards equipment.

Lyons was not a sympathetic employer. He did not understand his workers' demands, which caused a certain amount of tension, especially as his penny-pinching became increasingly blatant. In his view, everyone needed to make a big effort to make the company as successful as it was before the war, if not more so.

Clark Gable, Jaguar ambassador

In spite of everything, SS 100 cars returned to competition. Lyons himself would drive when he could, most notably with the driver John Ernest Appleyard, who would marry Lyons' daughter. Appleyard came third in the 1947 Coupe des Alpes. But it became clear by the end of the 1940s that Lyons' aim for Jaguar was to appeal to American customers. In 1948, Lyons left for a tour of the United States (as did the boss of the Triumph motorcycle brand, Edward Turner) and met Max Hoffman, who would become Jaguar's East Coast distributor in the US. The British cars were also put on display in Hollywood studios, where the actor Clark Gable bought a 3.5-litre Drophead Coupé. From then on, Gable would be one of Jaguar's most emblematic ambassadors. In 1953, Lyons ended his contract with Hoffman, who was also a distributor for Mercedes, one of Jaguar's biggest competitors. Jaguar Cars North American Corporation was then formed, to manage imports from Britain. Its cars quickly found favour with American customers.

Lord Garval and his wife acquired their SS Jaguar 3½ in 1939.

The bodies of the first Jaguars were polished with great care (here, Mark IVs from 1946).

On 12 February 1957, a large fire destroyed part of the plant. It almost ruined the career of the fledgling car manufacturer.

At Jaguar headquarters in Coventry, the engineers were kept busy. New models were on the drawing board, with William Heynes supervising their development. Robert Knight was taken on to design advanced suspension systems, then an essential component of comfort and roadholding, which was to become one of Jaguar's hallmarks. A triangulated system with telescopic dampers (shock absorbers) was developed for a chassis earmarked for the new Jaguar saloon, while Lyons took care of the design of the bodywork (later manufactured by Pressed Steel, one of Britain's biggest makers of panels). And so the Mark V was born – an odd designation, which required the previous 1½, 2½, and 3½ models to be retrospectively renamed the Mark IV. It was unveiled in 1948. However, it retained the old 2.5- and 3.5-litre six-cylinder engine, which was bought from Standard.

The big event of the late 1940s, however, was the development of the XK engine, the first made by Jaguar. The coming together of Lyons and Harry Weslake was essential to the birth of this project, even though Heynes and other Jaguar engineers (such as Claude Baily and Walter Hassan) took part in designing it. Weslake's scientific knowledge of the circulation of gases in internal combustion engines proved decisive. After some preliminary studies of four- and twelve-cylinder engines, the choice of design was quickly narrowed down to a six-cylinder unit. Although initially destined for the Mark V saloon, it appeared for the first time in the XK120, unveiled in 1948. The XK engine, in various sizes, was to power Jaguar cars until 1975. The XK120 was an immediate success, and contributed to the legendary status of the engine. It also enjoyed great success in competition, winning fame for Jaguar in races in the United States, France and even Cuba!

Glory at Le Mans

Despite all that, the XK's success did not curb Lyons' obsession with upmarket saloons and, in 1950, he unveiled the replacement for the Mark V: the Mark VII. This was followed by a more affordable saloon, powered by the 2.4-litre XK engine – the first Jaguar with a monocoque body (the chassis and bodywork built in one piece). Jaguar's success during the 1950s stemmed from Lyons' double ambition of wanting to produce prestigious cars at reasonable prices while demonstrating the marque's prowess in competition. The legendary Jaguar C-type and D-type were causing a sensation in the Le Mans 24 Hours, at a time when this race was followed all over the world.

Lyons was knighted in 1956, but the golden period that followed only lasted a year. In 1957, a terrible fire ravaged the factory at Browns Lane, Coventry, with 270 cars destroyed, including D-type and XKSS models destined for export to the United States (the road-going version of the D-type). Although no lives were lost, it cost the company more than £3m. But despite that, and through the determination of Sir William and his staff (numbering more than 4,000 people), the company was able to overcome this disaster and even unveil a new version of the 2.4-litre – the 3.4-litre – a few weeks after the fire. In the meantime, the XK120 had evolved into the XK140, to be followed by the XK150 at the end of the 1950s. The series of cars bearing the designation "Mark" was constantly extended, from the Mark VII to the smaller, superb Mark II.

In 1960, the Jaguar marque was expanded with the acquisition of Daimler, the oldest English car manufacturer (founded in 1896). By then, Lyons was getting on in years, something that was becoming the subject of jokes among his employees. He wanted to stop taking part in competitions and instead refocus Jaguar on large-scale production. Despite this, a team continued to work on technical developments for racing that would allow the E-type to replace the D-type. Over time, the E-type would become, above all, a sports model destined for use on the road – and perhaps the most famous car in the history of Jaguar.

1948

The unexpected success of the XK120 greatly boosted the popularity of the first Jaguar engine.

The Mark X prototype was tested in 1960 on the MIRA track, the world-famous test track that opened in 1946.

The final polishing of the Mark X was done by hand in 1962. Sir William Lyons attached great significance to this moment.

In 1950, the Mark V assembly lines, left, and those of the XK120, right, operated side by side.

Mark V
1948

The first Mark

After World War Two, Jaguar had to adapt to new markets and set its sights on the United States. The coachbuilder Cyril Holland, who had been with the company in the early days, had just left, as he was reluctant to use modern manufacturing methods. As a result, William Lyons became the sole boss and designer. Among the projects closest to his heart, replacing the 1.5-, 2.5- and 3.5-litre saloons (which had retrospectively been renamed the Mark IV) came top of the list. He also wanted to give the saloons more class, and decided not to fit them with the four-cylinder engine. The future Mark V (a name whose origins remain a mystery today) would feature the 2.6-litre and 3.5-litre six-cylinder engines, and not the new engine fitted to the XK120. The two cars were, incidentally, unveiled at the same time, at the 1948 London Motor Show at Earl's Court.

Lyons, together with William Heynes and Robert Knight, the two engineers who had worked with him on the Mark V, spent a long time studying the chassis and suspension system of the Bentley Mark VI. Those of the Jaguar Mark V were the result of this research.

The chassis used for the marque's older saloons was also improved, adopting the same arrangement as that of the Jaguar XK120, with two box sections, front suspension with torsion bars, leaf springs at the rear and hydraulic drum brakes. This chassis would serve until the 1950s, on the Mark VII and Mark VIII. The lines of the Mark V did not make a radical break with those of previous saloons, but the headlights were less prominent and the wheels smaller (41cm/16in), a sign of its modernity. The Mark V was replaced by the Mark VII in 1951.

OPPOSITE
While the XK120 outshone the Mark V in 1948, sales of the latter were much stronger.

===== **Jaguar Mark V 2.5, 1948** =====

DISPLACEMENT: inline six-cylinder, 2,663cc; **MAX POWER:** 102bhp; **TORQUE:** 133lb ft; naturally aspirated; rear-wheel drive; four-speed manual gearbox; **WEIGHT:** 1,700kg (3,748lb).

XK120
1948

Unexpected glory

OPPOSITE

"Half a loaf is better than none," as the saying goes. William Lyons had to think along similar lines when he hastily prepared a roadster (convertible), the future XK120, to make up for the absence of the Mark saloon, which he wanted to unveil at the 1948 Earl's Court Motor Show.

Who could have foreseen in 1948 that the Jaguar XK120 would leave such a mark on the brand's history? Surely no one – least of all William Lyons. The XK120 was not the result of chance but of a succession of unexpected decisions, taken in the heat of the moment. Following World War Two, Lyons knew that there were many markets the company had yet to enter (its sales until then had been essentially domestic). Opportunities needed to be created. Jaguar cars did not have an excellent reputation in North America, chiefly because of the difficulty of obtaining spare parts. Lyons took the time, in early 1948, to travel to the United States – a market of considerable size – to set up a dealer network. It was a smart move, for the XK120 was being launched that year, and would encounter international success.

Development of the new XK engine – the first to be designed entirely by Jaguar – had begun during World War Two. Harry Weslake, who had worked on the SS, and Claude Baily were joined by a gifted engine designer named Walter Hassan, while William Heynes, the chief engineer, oversaw the research. The team, which also included Charles Newcombe, worked relentlessly on the new engine, which, it was felt, should retain the six-cylinder configuration. Nevertheless, as work progressed, all kinds of possibilities were mooted, including a twelve-cylinder engine. Eventually, a four-cylinder unit with twin overhead camshafts was chosen in the first instance. Its displacement was increased and its output continually raised until it reached 105bhp. It was intended for a new Mark VII saloon. The tenth prototype of this four-cylinder engine to be produced was named the XJ, the first having been given the designation XA. The team eventually decided that the engine's power was too little to propel the heavy Mark VII, and therefore concluded that they needed to begin again, on a six-cylinder design. In September 1947, a 3.2-litre six-cylinder engine, named XJ6, was on the test stand. Most important was that maximum torque should be available at the lowest possible revs, since the engine was destined for a high-end saloon car. Thus displacement was increased to 3.4 litres by increasing the pistons' stroke length.

Although the engine seemed to be ready, the saloon's chassis had yet to be designed, and there

KWR 264

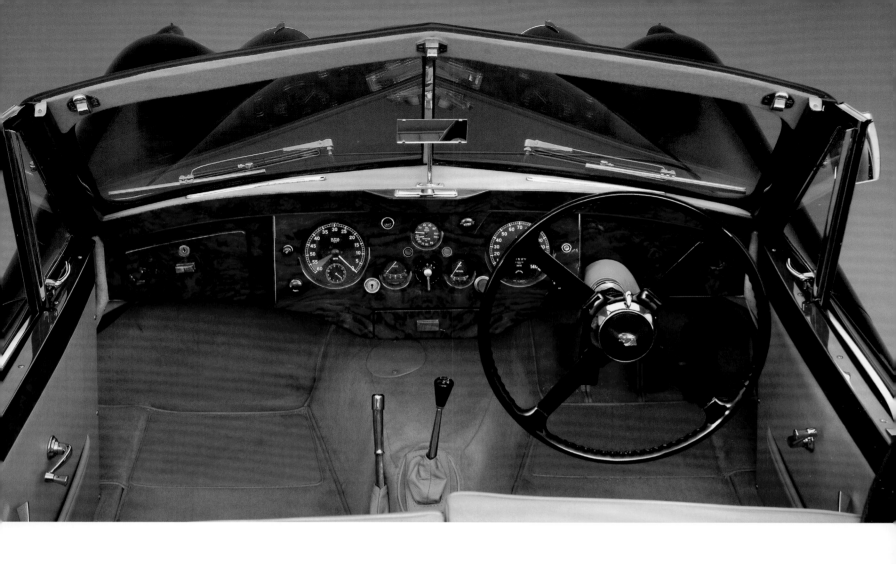

XK120

The XK120 was replaced by the XK140 in 1954, six years after its impromptu release.

OPPOSITE, TOP
In order to be ready for the Earl's Court Motor Show, William Lyons bolted an aluminium body over an existing wooden model, without recourse to additional plans.

OPPOSITE, BOTTOM
The double windscreen (windshield) was reminiscent of the pre-war period. On the other hand, the engine, designed in 1942, foreshadowed innovations to come.

ABOVE
Unlike this more recent XK120, the dashboard of the original 1948 XK120 was not wooden. It was covered in Connolly leather, which was commonly used on chairs.

ABOVE
A Fixed-head Coupé (FHC) was released in 1951 with a permanent roof. The XK120 was entered into competitions where it met with widespread success.

RIGHT
The XK120 six-cyclinder was intended for the Mark V saloon, but Lyons thought its power underwhelming, so he opted to introduce this engine in a roadster.

were only a few months to go until the 1948 London Motor Show. Lyons was thinking of a prototype based on a shortened Mark V chassis as the setting for the new six-cylinder engine so that it could be exhibited at the show. Lyons hastily designed a sporty body made from aluminium panels. Job done. The XK120 Super Sport was born. Only 200 were to be built but, given the new car's popularity with press and public alike, orders were not long in coming. Boasting 160bhp, with lines that were both elegant and sporty, wheels borrowed from Jaguar's saloons, thin chrome bumpers and an aluminium body, the XK120 had nailed it. Caught flat-footed, Jaguar hurried to equip the factory with machine tools that could mass-produce the XK120.

The XK120 subsequently enjoyed several successes in competition, and was sought-after by the biggest international stars.

XK120

The XK120 appeared on screen many times, including in the *Batman* (1966) TV series.

Jaguar XK120, 1948

DISPLACEMENT: inline six-cylinder, 3,442cc; **MAX POWER:** 160bhp; **TORQUE:** 195lb ft; naturally aspirated; rear-wheel drive; four-speed manual gearbox; **WEIGHT:** 1,320kg (2,910lb).

C-Type
1951

A focus on endurance

OPPOSITE
In order to reduce its weight, the C-type's body was made of aluminium, while its chassis was made of aluminium tubing.

In 1951, Jaguar decided to offer customers a race-oriented version of the XK120. However, it was not simply a matter of relaunching the same car, but rather of offering a real race car. This was the C-type, otherwise known as the XJ120-C. While the XK120 was noted for its rather angular roadster shape, the C-type had the look of a small boat, with rounded lines and boasting a superb convex front end and a breathtaking outline, creating a fluidity almost unmatched at the time. The design came from the pen of Malcolm Sayer, Jaguar's aerodynamics specialist, who had done a great deal of work on the fast car's balance. To save weight, engineers gave the C-type an aluminium body and a tubular chassis. The car was also innovative in its rack-and-pinion steering, which was much lighter and more precise than on the production XK120.

As far as the engine was concerned, the C-type logically inherited the XK120's 3.4-litre unit. This was an inline six-cylinder engine that had undergone a few modifications to the valve springs, camshaft and carburettors. The designers had managed to make its power leap from 160 to 205bhp. Its most recent incarnation, dating from 1954, was made lighter by more than 50kg (110lb), and it gained a further 15bhp, making a total of 220bhp. Following two victories at the Le Mans 24 Hours (in 1951 and 1953), the C-type remains one of the most legendary cars in the history of the automobile. Only 53 C-types ever left the Coventry factory.

Jaguar C-Type, 1951

DISPLACEMENT: inline six-cylinder, 3,442cc; **MAX POWER:** 205bhp; **TORQUE:** 220lb ft.; rear-wheel drive; four-speed manual gearbox; **WEIGHT:** 941kg (2,075lb).

The C-type and D-type won five victories at
the Le Mans 24 Hours between 1951 and 1957.

The triumph of the cat

| 1951 |

At the start of the 1950s, the XK120 was enjoying huge success. William Lyons wanted to produce a racing version of his roadster for endurance events. His goal was to take part in the 1951 Le Mans 24 Hours. With William Heynes, Lyons' chief engineer, and his team, Jaguar prepared a car in barely six months. Its name was the XK120-C, renamed the C-type.

Jaguar entered no fewer than three cars in the Le Mans 24 Hours of 1951. Faced with the C-type, Aston Martin were ready to do battle with their DB2. For most of the race, the Jaguars were in the lead, but only one of them, No. 20, could maintain an average speed of 93mph to win the event.

In 1952, Mercedes was dominant with its 300 SL, which was more powerful. However, the following year, now equipped with four disc brakes, the C-type regained the upper hand, and Jaguar finished in first, second and fourth place at Le Mans. After Ferrari won in 1954, Jaguar won the race three years running with the D-type. After that, the British big cat would return to Le Mans, but not until much later…

RIGHT
Peter Whitehead and Peter Walker won first place at the Le Mans 24 Hours in 1951, driving a C-type. This marked the first victory won at the wheel of this car.

Mark VII
1950

Grand luxury

OPPOSITE
The Mark VII initially
came with a four-speed
manual gearbox.
It later became
available with an
automatic gearbox.

The saloons designed by William Lyons very quickly came to rival the most famous luxury cars of the day, including those from Rolls-Royce and Bentley. Indeed, it was because of the Bentley Mark VI, which had been launched in 1946, that the luxurious Jaguar following the Mark V was named the Mark VII, not the Mark VI, when it was launched four years later.

Production of the Mark VII was seriously delayed. The difficulty of sourcing steel after the war, which affected Jaguar's supplier Pressed Steel, as well as a few internal problems at Jaguar itself, explain why the Mark VII was not unveiled until October 1950, at the Earl's Court Motor Show in London. The car featured the XK six-cylinder engine that had been fitted to the XK120 for the past two years (see page 28), without any modifications. Nevertheless, two versions were available, with different compression ratios, to suit the petrol sold in different countries, the quality of which could be highly unpredictable. The chassis was little changed from that of its predecessor, the Mark V, retaining the same wheelbase of 10ft (3.08m). The bodywork, on the other hand, had

been completely redesigned. The Mark VII was tall and broad, fitting all the criteria for early 1950s luxury and comfort. The end of the bonnet (hood) flaunted a jaguar's head, flanked by outspread wings. The rear wheels were covered by the bodywork, which was de rigueur for an elegant car at the time, both in Britain and elsewhere, clearly indicating the kind of customer it was aimed at. Lyons had ambitions for the big saloon in America – he had been targeting this important market since the aftermath of the war and saw the Mark VII as the ideal car for entering it. He was not mistaken.

The 160bhp six-cylinder engine was more than enough to allow the Mark VII to claim the title of highest-performance touring car of its time; at its launch in 1950, it had a top speed of 100mph and also benefited from the image of the XK120. The Mark VII had a comfortable interior and excellent roadholding, but its braking came in for some criticism, despite being fitted with power brakes. This did not prevent orders from flooding in – Lyons was forced to acquire new premises in order to boost production.

ABOVE
The pure, rounded style of
the Mark VII was proof of
the genius of William Lyons,
who designed all his cars.

RIGHT
Despite its lavish
appearance, the Mark VII
participated in the Monte
Carlo Rally of 1956. Shown
here in 1963.

The Mark VII was developed rapidly. It became the first Jaguar to be available with an optional BorgWarner automatic gearbox, as unveiled at the 1953 New York Motor Show. The Mark VII M, distinguished by its wider bumpers, arrived the following year, featuring the same engine but with its output increased by 30bhp.

More surprisingly, the Mark VII took part in many competitions, thanks to its engine's grunt and in spite of its hefty weight. At the 1952 Monte Carlo Rally, a Mark VII narrowly missed making it onto the podium. The following year, several Jaguar Mark VIIs were on the starting line of that prestigious event.

Ian Ernest Appleyard and his wife Patricia (Lyons' daughter) came second, behind a Ford Zephyr driven by Peter Worledge and Maurice Gatsonides. In 1954, Jaguar built a special lightweight version, fitted with the D-type's engine and Dunlop brakes, and with some parts of the body in magnesium, but this car never took part in a competition.

In 1956, the Mark VII made way for the Mark VIII – extending the life of the six-cylinder engine, now producing 210bhp and shared with the XK140. Its interior reached new heights of luxury, establishing Jaguar saloons at the very top of high-end cars.

Mark VII
The Mark VII became very popular in the United States, the world's largest market.

Jaguar Mark VII, 1950

DISPLACEMENT: inline six-cylinder, 3,442cc; **MAX POWER:** 160bhp; **TORQUE:** 195lb ft; naturally aspirated; rear-wheel drive; four-speed manual gearbox or automatic; **WEIGHT:** 1,660kg (3,660lb).

D-Type
1954

A new era in design

OPPOSITE
D-types came in many different versions with three different spoiler options and a variety of hood (convertible top) lengths.

Even though Jaguar won the Le Mans 24 Hours in 1953, the manufacturer decided to replace the C-type with a new car: the C-type Mark II, which would eventually be renamed the D-type. The aim was to deepen the commitment to endurance racing. In 1954, the manufacturer unveiled a new boat-shaped car that also emphasized rounded lines, but Malcolm Sayer went back to the drawing board to come up with a more horizontal shape. Gone was the rounded bonnet of the early 1950s. The latter half of the decade was ushered in with a line that was slimmer, especially at the front of the car. Two large convex headlights extended along a bonnet that had been made more slender at its centre. At the rear, the design was sharper and featured a fin whose function was to increase aerodynamic stability at high speed.

With the D-type, Sayer, who had also worked on its predecessor, produced an even more attractive design. The lines of the C-type were undeniably pleasing, but it must be admitted that the styling of the D-type is one of the most beautiful in the history of Jaguar. Thanks to its light weight and power output of up to 250bhp, the car was also famous for its performance. It could reach 60mph in just 4.7 seconds (a real feat in the 1950s) and attain a top speed of up to 162mph. Among the innovations on the D-type were four disc brakes – it was one of the few cars of its generation to have them. The Jaguar D-type was to distinguish itself repeatedly in endurance races, notably at Le Mans. The next logical step would be the arrival of the E-type in 1961…

Jaguar D-Type, 1954

DISPLACEMENT: inline six-cylinder, 3,442cc; **MAX POWER:** 250bhp; **TORQUE:** 242lb ft; rear-wheel drive; four-speed manual gearbox; **WEIGHT:** 875kg (1,929lb).

XKSS
1957

The collector's piece

The Jaguar D-type performed outstandingly in endurance racing but Sir William Lyons decided to withdraw from competition at the end of the 1956 season, leaving a number of D-type cars unsold at the Browns Lane factory. Lyons had the idea of converting these racing cars into "street-legal" vehicles (regulations were a far cry from those of today). He was also inspired by the work of the driver Duncan Hamilton, who had previously prepared a D-type for road use.

In order to recoup some of the investment made producing the unused chassis and to exploit the lucrative American market for European sports cars, Lyons decided to carry out only a few minor modifications to these D-types: the addition of a door on the passenger side; the removal of the large tailfin; and the elimination of the partition between the passenger and driver's seats. Further improvements were made for both aesthetic and legal reasons: a full-width, chrome-rimmed windscreen (which came from the Ford Consul); a folding fabric top, offering rudimentary protection from the elements; chrome bumpers front and rear (later used on the E-type); rear lights from

the XK140, which were mounted higher on the wings; and fine chrome strips around the front headlamps. All that remained was to come up with a name, and that was the XK Super Sport.

Work began at the end of 1956. The price was set at $6,900, which was relatively reasonable at the time compared to cars by Mercedes and Ferrari. The engine – the XK's 3.4-litre six-cylinder unit fitted with a reworked cylinder head and three Weber carburettors – produced 250bhp at 5,700 rpm, and its aluminium body kept the weight below a tonne, meaning that the XKSS could reach 143mph, a considerable speed at the time. Fortunately, its excellent braking system, with four Dunlop discs, quickly reined in the engine's exuberance. All this pointed to healthy sales, helped by the D-type's pedigree and the superb lines of the XKSS. However, a major unforeseen event intervened.

On the evening of 12 February 1957, a fire broke out at the Browns Lane factory. It destroyed nine of the twenty-five cars that had been completed, or almost. The remaining 16 all found buyers in the United States, including one acquired by the

ABOVE
The XKSS combined brute
speed – due to its race
track origins – with 1950s
elegance.

RIGHT
The XK's 3,442cc six-cylinder
engine was fuelled by
three carburettors. The XKSS
served as the guinea pig
for the E-type.

actor and amateur pilot Steve McQueen, who was crazy about this kind of car.

The XKSS's rarity and its unusual history rapidly turned it into a legendary car – to the point that, for 2016, Jaguar asked its Classic division to build nine cars to replace those that had been destroyed in the fire, following the original specifications but adapting them to modern standards. Each car was made by hand – this required 10,000 hours of labour per car – after models from the time had been analysed to discover the secrets of how they were built. Naturally, the price for each car reflected this – it exceeded £1m ($1.27m). Nevertheless, all nine cars found satisfied buyers. The 16 XKSS cars from 1957 remain in private hands. There is no doubt, though, that this sort of excess enhanced the already glittering image of Jaguar and its unique status.

XKSS

The XKSS had all the trappings of a legendary car. Celebrities, like Steve McQueen, quickly caught on.

Jaguar XKSS, 1957

DISPLACEMENT: inline six-cylinder, 3,442cc; **MAX POWER:** 250bhp; **TORQUE:** 242lb ft; naturally aspirated; rear-wheel drive; four-speed manual gearbox; **WEIGHT:** 990kg (1,98lb).

XK140
1955

America

The XK120, created in haste in 1948, experienced a rebirth with the XK140, which was unveiled at the end of 1954 (making it a 1955 model). The XK140's modifications were aimed essentially at the American market, the world's biggest at that time – all car manufacturers dreamed of getting themselves a place in the sun of California or Texas or in New York. The Jaguar XK140 was produced until 1957, when it was replaced by the Jaguar XK150.

The bulkier bumpers were the external feature that most clearly set the XK140 apart from the XK120, together with a grille that had broader bars, and chrome trim strips on the bonnet and boot (trunk). The basic engine was still the inline six-cylinder 3.4-litre unit, fitted with a double SU H6 carburettor, which had a maximum power output of 190bhp at 5,500 rpm – up from 180bhp for the XK120 SE – thanks to a few modifications.

Although very similar to its predecessor, the XK140 was improved in several ways, especially with regard to comfort and driver enjoyment. The XK120 was a sports car, while the XK140 was less sporty but more luxurious. Racing equipment was no longer even offered as an option, but it was still possible to request it by special order, as always with Jaguar.

The interior was trimmed with leather, right up to the comprehensive dashboard. The door panels were shorter than those of the XK120. The engine was set some 4in (10cm) further forward, which noticeably increased the space for passengers, offering more legroom and a better driving position. There was rack-and-pinion steering and more effective suspension.

All these modifications were applied to the three body styles: roadster, fixed-head (two-door) coupé and drophead (convertible) coupé.

Overdrive (a higher top gear for driving on major roads) was offered as an option, as were wire wheels and a radio. Three-speed automatic transmission was available from 1956, making the XK140 the first Jaguar sports car to feature an automatic gearbox.

Like the 120, the 140 SE (known as 140 M in the US) featured wire wheels, fog lights and dual exhausts. The C-type option, with two HS8 carburettors, attained a power output of 210bhp.

OPPOSITE
The XK140 Fixed-head Coupé was cheaper than the drophead versions, but not as good looking.

ABOVE
In a way, the XK140 Roadster prolonged the life of the SS1 series. The spoked rims were typical of the era.

RIGHT
The 1950s coupés and roadsters were not known for their spaciousness. Their steering wheels were often bulky.

The XK140 took part in competitions discreetly, achieving second place in the British RAC Rally in 1956, but the D-type stole the limelight and eclipsed the few exploits of the coupé.

In 1957, almost ten years after the launch of the XK120, the oldest member of the family, Jaguar unveiled the XK150. Radically different from its predecessors, its lines were softened and the one-piece windscreen was curved – the same as the rear window in the coupé. Mechanically, the biggest difference was the introduction of disc brakes, which had first appeared on Jaguar cars at Le Mans in 1954. The engine was the same 3.4-litre unit, producing 190bhp in its basic version and 220bhp in the SE version, which was fitted with bigger carburettors. Initially, the 150 was launched as a fixed-head coupé and a drophead coupé; a roadster came out in 1958. More than just a development, the 150 was a modern car; but it did not create a sensation like its illustrious predecessor, the XK120.

XK140
The XK140 Jaguar targeted the highly coveted American market.

Jaguar XK140, 1955

DISPLACEMENT: inline six-cylinder, 3,342cc; **MAX POWER:** 190bhp; **TORQUE:** 210lb ft; naturally aspirated; rear-wheel drive; four-speed manual gearbox; **WEIGHT:** 1,422kg (3,135lb).

The initial SS often overheated during its first rallies.
The issue was later resolved.

Races for the people

| 1932 - 1968 |

From the 1900s onward, the general public keenly followed motor rallies. These events crisscrossed minor roads in the countries where they were held, showcasing the reliability of the cars, and were covered at length in the press.

The SS marque, which became Jaguar in 1945, quickly got involved. Some SS Tourers took part in a few English rallies. In 1933, three of them, prepared for the purpose, lined up at the start for the Coupe des Alpes, a famous European event which, that year, ran from Merano in northern Italy to Nice, France. But the engines quickly became hot, which limited their performance. Nevertheless, they came in the top 12 in the final classification.

Success came in 1948 with the SS 100, driven by Ian Ernest Appleyard. In domestic rallies, William Lyons sometimes drove one of his cars himself. Jaguar relentlessly promoted its image through rallying until the 1960s, sometimes entering its large saloons, such as the enormous Mark V cars, in the Monte Carlo Rally, and its Mark 2 cars in the Tour de France Automobile.

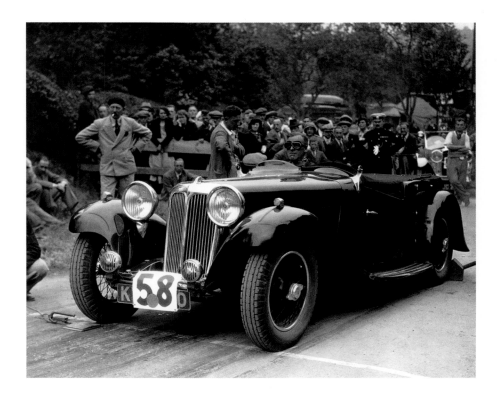

ABOVE
Hans Georg Koch raced the International Alpine Trial in 1933 with an SS1 (No. 38), alongside Peter Orssich, who drove an SS1 Coupé (No. 39). They encountered multiple problems.

Mark I
1955

Top-of-the-range family car

OPPOSITE
The 2.4-litre Mark I was the first monocoque Jaguar.

It was in September 1955 that the 2.4-litre saloon was unveiled, a successor to the 1.5- and 2.5-litre saloons of 1949. In 1959, it was retrospectively renamed Mark I, to distinguish it from the new Mark II.

Although William Lyons had initially intended to produce a four-door saloon based on the XK120, he quickly had to change his plans for financial reasons. The unitary body shell was greatly modified, but the suspension was more traditional for the time, featuring double wishbones and coil springs. The rear axle used a simplified version of the D-type suspension, with inverted semi-elliptic springs.

The engine was a smaller-capacity version of the six-cylinder 3.4-litre unit from the XK120, with a maximum power output of 112bhp, which made the Mark I a performance saloon. From 1956, Jaguar offered, as an option, a version of the 2.4-litre engine that produced 150bhp. In 1957 another version appeared, with the 3.4-litre engine from the Mark VIII, which produced 210bhp and was aimed primarily at the American market. The Jaguar 3.4 litre had a larger radiator grille for better cooling, and a sturdier rear axle. However, a fire at the Browns Lane factory – the same that put paid to the XKSS – disrupted production.

In September 1957, a BorgWarner three-speed automatic transmission (formerly an option restricted to cars for export) was offered for both the 2.4- and 3.4-litre engines, as well as Dunlop disc brakes on all four wheels.

=== **Jaguar Mark I, 1955** ===

DISPLACEMENT: inline six-cylinder, 2,483cc; **MAX POWER:** 112bhp; **TORQUE:** 140lb ft; naturally aspirated; rear-wheel drive; four-speed manual gearbox; **WEIGHT:** 1,400kg (3,086lb).

Mark VIII
1956

An obsession with luxury

In 1954, the Mark VII M – a development of the Mark VII – arrived, followed in 1956 by the Mark VIII. Sir William Lyons (who was knighted in the same year), was obsessed with the market for luxury cars aimed at well-heeled buyers. As a result, the various Mark designations that succeeded each other during this period did not feature any extraordinary innovations – Lyons had learned to be wary of radical transformations, which had sometimes almost cost his company its life because of problems with subcontractors.

The Mark VIII inherited the XK140's six-cylinder engine, featuring a "B" type cylinder head and larger-diameter valves, as well as an exhaust designed accordingly. These modifications improved mid-range torque, while retaining a power output that was respectable for the time (210bhp).

Outwardly, the Mark VIII was recognizable by its one-piece windscreen, which was more modern than the two-piece windscreen in the Mark VII. The headlights were different, too, and a strip of chrome trim divided the body into two sections, which were painted in different colours. A small figurine of a jaguar about to jump topped the new radiator grille. The rear wheels were more visible – another concession to modernity. The interior fittings were more luxurious; cars with an automatic gearbox had a bench-type front seat, whereas those with manual transmission had individual seats. Only the last two models produced had power steering.

When production ceased, in 1958, slightly more than 6,000 Mark VIII cars had been sold. According to the international Mark VIII Register, only 158 are still in existence today.

OPPOSITE
The Mark VIII and the first version of the Mark IX that succeeded it were hard to tell apart from the exterior.

Jaguar Mark VIII, 1956

DISPLACEMENT: inline six-cylinder, 3,442cc; **MAX POWER:** 210bhp; **TORQUE:** 215lb ft; naturally aspirated; rear-wheel drive; four-speed manual gearbox or automatic; **WEIGHT:** 1,702kg (3,752lb).

Birth of a legend:
The Jaguar E-Type

1961 › 1974

The launch of the Jaguar E-type in 1961 was like a thunderbolt, the effects of which are still in evidence today. The E-type is likely to remain the most famous Jaguar in the marque's history.

Just after the D-type's three victories in the Le Mans 24 Hours (from 1955 to 1957), work on the future E-type began. From a technical point of view, the car could not disappoint: four disc brakes, independent suspension with telescopic dampers at the rear, inboard brakes against the rear differential, monocoque construction with a tubular subframe carrying the engine at the front, 3.8-litre XK engine with twin overhead camshafts…Its only weakness was its sluggish Moss gearbox but that was, fortunately, replaced later. Its price was on a par with the comfortable saloons of the time – and half that of the Ferraris and Lamborghinis with which it was competing. Finally, its superb lines – the work of Malcolm Sayer and Sir William Lyons – led Enzo Ferrari to say, at the E-type's unveiling in Geneva in 1961: "That is the most beautiful car in the world!" Its immensely long bonnet set it apart from all other sports cars, along with its passenger compartment, whose rounded shape was as elegant as it was original (though to the detriment of comfort).

Everything was in place for the E-type to leave its mark on history. From the time of its launch, it had a place on the starting grid of English racetracks. The famous racing driver Graham Hill won a race

in the spring of 1961 driving a completely standard E-type. Race-car preparers quickly got their hands on the Jaguar in order to improve it. The Briggs Cunningham racing team finished fourth in the Le Mans 24 Hours in 1962 with an E-type Lightweight. The following year Jaguar produced 12 lightweight versions of the large coupé. The car's body, made entirely of aluminium, housed an engine based on the 3.8-litre unit of the production car, but in aluminium, not cast iron. These cars were fast, but unreliable. The factory reverted to the cast-iron engine, tuned to produce 300bhp, with which it had more success. The most powerful E-type was probably that of racing driver Peter Lindner. He competed in the Le Mans 24 Hours in 1964 in his Lightweight, whose engine, prepared by the engineer Samir Klat, produced 350bhp. Lindner was sadly killed a few months later on the French Montlhéry circuit, at its wheel.

A muddled approach

Saloon cars were not neglected, and the Mark X arrived at just the right time, in 1961, to replace the overly discreet Mark IX. Like the E-type, it inherited the first 3.8-litre six-cylinder engine. Tests were conducted with a view to fit the car with a V8 and even a V12, but this would have required designing a new chassis, and development of the Mark X had already been very costly.

One of the Beatles, George Harrison, was unable to resist the charm of the E-type.

The Browns Lane plant reached maximum production capacity in the 1960s. It soon merged with the British Motor Corporation (BMC).

The first E-type assembly lines, built in 1961, were narrow, especially for a car with such a long bonnet.

The unveiling of the E-type has gone down in the history of the automobile: few cars have made such a splash.

The less opulent 3.4-litre S and 3.8-litre S, unveiled in 1963 and quickly named the S-type, completed the Jaguar range. Only the latter was exported to the United States, which was always an important market for Jaguar. The following year, the Mark X was fitted with the 4.2-litre XK engine, an essential for American customers, who were fond of big engines.

During the second half of the 1960s, Jaguar lost its way somewhat, being too eager to introduce novelties. The 420, a sort of slightly facelifted Mark X, arrived in 1966, and was also available in a Daimler Sovereign version. Then came the smaller 240 and 340 in 1967, and the Daimler 250 V8. Although these cars proved to be excellent, they slightly confused the visibility of the Jaguar range, as did the arrival of the imposing DS420, the favourite limousine of royal families from 1968 onward. What was needed was a flagship saloon that embodied the luxury and performance so emblematic of the marque.

Research and development had begun in 1961, just after the unveiling of the E-type in Geneva. Lyons was demanding a comfortable car based on the chassis of the E-type, and that offered more room. A prototype was quickly built and named the XJ4 – the first in a long series. However, keeping to the dimensions of the E-type made it impossible to fulfil the boss's wishes regarding space. The engineer William Heynes suggested building two versions: one enlarged for the United States, the other with E-type dimensions for Europe. And so the XJ6 was born, the other star in Jaguar's history. Heynes, incidentally, retired a year after its appearance. Several engines were considered, from a six-cylinder to a V12, but when it was launched, in 1968, the XJ6 featured the XK engines, either 2.8 litres or 4.2 litres. Its shape was inspired by the 420. Its rear axle was from the E-type, but the front axle was improved. In 1969, the Daimler Sovereign – an XJ6 with a different badge – was launched. The XJ6 had been ready since 1966, but Jaguar had to wait until the panel manufacturer Pressed Steel, with which the company had worked for a long time, had set up the tools to produce the XJ models. When it was launched, delivery times were still very long,

putting off some customers. The entry-level model, with the 2.8-litre engine, cost £1,800 – once again, a competitive price. Commercial success was not long in coming.

Future prospects

Such a rosy picture might suggest that Jaguar was in excellent financial health, which was not far from the truth. But Britain's car industry was experiencing major difficulties, which would not improve during the 1970s. Mergers were very much in vogue at the time, according to the principle that there is strength in numbers. In 1952, the Austin and Morris marques merged to become the British Motor Corporation (BMC). BMC later acquired the bodywork manufacturer Pressed Steel, one of Jaguar's biggest subcontractors. There was only one more step to take: BMC acquired Jaguar in July 1966.

For the first time in its history, and in spite of the dominant figure of Lyons, Jaguar had lost its independence. That said, the company was already listed on the stock exchange and subject to the influence of its shareholders, but Lyons was the sole person in charge when it came to important decisions. From 1966, though, this was no longer the case. Why did he agree to the acquisition? There were several reasons. He was getting on in years and had no heir (his only son had been killed in a car accident), and perhaps he thought that his company would be on a firmer footing. Furthermore, belonging to a group that owned Pressed Steel seemed logical. Finally, the launch of the XJ6 required substantial investment in manufacturing tools, funding that BMC could provide, and there were also opportunities for rationalizing production.

But, at the end of the 1960s – and despite the new acquisition of the truck manufacturer Leyland by the group, which became British Leyland Motor Corporation (BLMC) – financial difficulties arose. The decisions made by various managers, the launch of certain ill-advised models by Austin and Morris and the running of this big group, which wanted to follow the example of its American counterparts, explain the failures that were to come.

1966
The Jaguar series had been utterly lost before the release of the XJ6.

The Mark X underwent extensive development. No Jaguar had been put through so many tests.

An odd mix of cars could be found at the Browns Lane site in the 1960s.

The Daimler DS420 pointed the automaker in the right direction, but Sir William Lyons always made sure Daimlers never overshadowed Jaguars.

E-Type

When the E-type was launched in Geneva, Enzo Ferrari said it was the most beautiful car in the world.

OPPOSITE, TOP
The E-type was immediately released as a coupé and a convertible, and a little later, as a 2+2 (a coupé with two small back seats). Production began in 1961 and ended in 1975.

OPPOSITE, BOTTOM
Sir William Lyons is visibly relaxed as he poses for the camera in front of an E-type, launched in Geneva in 1961. The car had only just been delivered the day before.

ABOVE
This 1968 4.2-litre E-type interior embodies English pomp. The Series 2 began production the same year, incorporating a few cosmetic modifications and new brakes.

ABOVE
More than 72,000 E-types were produced between 1961 and 1975. The Series 2 was the most suited to the road.

RIGHT
The E-type V12 captured the attention of the media as well as public adoration at the 1971 Earl's Court Motor Show.

its modern chassis delighted and its price was amazingly reasonable compared to its competitors (it was half the price of a Ferrari). Yet again, the rich and famous placed orders immediately.

The 3.8-litre six-cylinder produced a claimed 265bhp at 5,500 rpm, but its design (it had a long stroke) favoured torque. The early models had a four-speed manual gearbox (first was not synchronized).

The E-type could easily whisk its driver beyond 140mph, and its roadholding was among the best – without compromising on comfort.

In 1964, the 3.8-litre engine made way for a 4.2-litre six-cylinder unit. From 1971, the E-type was powered by an enormous 5.3-litre V12 in aluminium but, sadly, its reliability was not bulletproof. Production ended in 1975.

E-Type

The E-type's V12 engine produced almost 280bhp.

Jaguar E-Type, 1961

DISPLACEMENT: inline six-cylinder, 3,781cc; **MAX POWER:** 265hp; **TORQUE:** 260lb ft; naturally aspirated; rear-wheel drive; four-speed manual gearbox; **WEIGHT:** 1,275kg (2,811lb).

Mark X
1961

Opulence

OPPOSITE

In 1961, after the successful release of the E-type and the triumph of the Mark II, Jaguar turned its attention to the new Mark X. But the public, particularly the American public, did not appreciate this classic type.

The Mark X was launched in the same year as the E-type, making 1961 a productive year for Jaguar. It was innovative in several ways: it had independent rear suspension, four disc brakes, a monocoque chassis and more. It inherited the XK's 3.8-litre six-cylinder engine, which was also in the E-type. Its three-speed gearbox could, as an option, be replaced by an automatic.

The Mark X demanded a lot from its engineers, including a great deal of development and testing, which took place on the famous English MIRA test track, used by various British car manufacturers. Sir William Lyons' target audience for the Mark X was VIPs – kings, queens, diplomats, heads of government and so on – and the car's generous proportions were meant to embody the importance of the world's elite. Jaguar's modern look, with four headlights set into rounded front wings, made its first appearance on the Mark X. Nothing had been left to chance in the design of the interior, from the vanity mirrors to the radio and the picnic tables for the rear passengers. Rolls-Royce had better watch out. All the more so since, like for like, Jaguar's offerings cost half the price.

Boasting 265bhp, this large saloon was not scared of breaking the 120mph barrier – a considerable achievement for a car weighing 2 tonnes, at a time when the Citroën DS struggled to hit 90mph. Its stable handling, which was balanced and precise, was impressive in a car of its size. However, in the US, it was criticized for a certain sluggishness – American customers were accustomed to more vigour from a Jaguar. This was bad news, because the Mark X was aimed above all at the American market. Accordingly, for several years the model suffered from a discrepancy between what it promised and what it delivered. Brochures showed movie stars (actually lookalikes) in the most glamorous settings. But the Mark X sometimes found itself in the hands of less respectable people, who took advantage of its performance to travel to places where certain kinds of business were conducted with the greatest discretion.

Its handling invited a certain amount of excess. The Mark X was the first Jaguar saloon to be offered with independent rear suspension. It employed a wider version of the unit that had appeared for the first time on the E-type, and which was subsequently

ABOVE
In late 1964, Jaguar replaced the 3.8-litre 6-cylinder of the Mark X with a 4.2-litre engine. Two years later, at the London Motor Show, it unveiled the 420G, the new and improved Mark X.

RIGHT
The opulent interior, complete with wooden dashboard, rivalled that of Rolls-Royce. In 1964, the Mark X received a new 4-speed gearbox. It was also available with a Borg Warner automatic gearbox.

fitted to all Jaguar cars until production of the XJS in 1996. The front suspension used double wishbones with coil springs and telescopic dampers.

The arrival of the 4.2-litre engine in 1964 coincided with the introduction of a newly developed, fully synchronized, four-speed gearbox, to replace the old gearbox of the XK. However, many cars for the British market, and almost all cars destined for the North American market, left the factory with a BorgWarner automatic gearbox.

In October 1966, the Mark X was renamed the Jaguar 420G (not to be confused with the Jaguar 420). Visually, the difference between the 420G and the Mark X was the addition of a vertical central bar dividing the radiator grille into two halves. A "limousine" version was also available, with a lengthened wheelbase, glass partition between the rear passengers and driver, and a bench replacing the seats on the standard model. This was built until 1992.

Mark X

The Mark X was marketed to the rich and famous, from kings to movie stars.

Jaguar Mark X, 1961

DISPLACEMENT: inline six-cylinder, 3,781cc; **MAX POWER:** 265bhp; **TORQUE:** 260lb ft; naturally aspirated; rear-wheel drive; four-speed manual gearbox or automatic; **WEIGHT:** 1,880kg (4,145lb).

XJ13
1966

Shooting star

OPPOSITE
This design allowed the
XJ13 to accommodate
a V12 that produced
more than 500hp.

In 1960, Jaguar came up with the idea of manufacturing a car with a rear mid-engine that could compete in races but also be approved for the road. Regulations required participants in the Le Mans 24 Hours to register 50 copies of each race model for road use. Jaguar's initial objective was to develop a mid-mounted V12, since the Ford GT40 and various mid-engine Ferraris were clearly outpacing front-engined GT cars.

In 1966, the company unveiled the XJ13 prototype, a roadster, with lines that were both pure and rounded. This stroke of genius came from Malcolm Sayer, the designer and aerodynamicist who had given the world the C-type, D-type and E-type (and the JS, to boot). Under the engine cover of the XJ13, he joined and mounted two XK six-cylinder blocks to make a twelve-cylinder engine. The 5-litre V12 put out 509bhp on its first test run. While this power may have seemed very high at the time, the XJ13 was also quite heavy, weighing 1,125kg (2,478lb). Moreover, it took longer to develop than the Ferrari or Ford cars, and the project was quickly abandoned due to time constraints and lack of means. In 1971, the car was completely destroyed during the shooting of an advertisement at the MIRA test circuit. It was later rebuilt from scratch. Jaguar only built one XJ13 model, but a few "tribute" replicas were created by industry experts. As for the original XJ13, it is now owned by Jaguar.

Jaguar XJ13, 1966

DISPLACEMENT: V12, 4,994cc; **MAX POWER:** 509hp, **TORQUE:** 386lb ft; naturally aspirated; rear-wheel drive; five-speed manual gearbox; **WEIGHT:** 1,125kg (2,478lb).

Daimler
Motor Company

1960

The emblem

OPPOSITE

Starting with the V8 250 and the Sovereign, Daimlers effectively became Jaguars by a new name, until 2009. This XJ12-based Daimler Double-Six ceased production in 1997.

In 1960, Jaguar purchased the well-known marque Daimler. Contrary to popular belief, the Daimler Motor Company by then had nothing to do with the German Daimler Motoren Gesellschaft company, which had been founded by Gottlieb Daimler when the first automobiles were being built at the end of the 19th century. He later renamed his company Daimler Mercedes Benz, after his partnership with Carl Benz. In 1896, Frederick Richard Simms decided to buy the patent for the UK from Gottlieb Daimler.

The Daimler Motor Company in the UK began to manufacture luxury cars, to the point where it became the preferred vehicle supplier to the British royal family. But in the 1950s, Norah Docker, the wife of Daimler's director, Sir Bernard Docker, was reproached for her extravagance, especially regarding company assets. The royal family put an end to its collaboration with Daimler and turned instead to a brand that was felt to be more in line with aristocratic values: Rolls-Royce. After Docker was let go, Daimler's sales plunged, and the last attempt at manufacturing a sports car, the SP250, was a commercial failure.

But let us return to the Jaguar era. Sir William Lyons did not buy Daimler in order to manufacture more cars. Rather, the Daimler name allowed him to add high-end finishing touches to his forthcoming models. He indulged in the creation of an emblem, which appeared for the first time on the Mark II. Lyons took advantage of his purchase of Daimler to install the V8 from the Daimler 250 in his superb saloon. Soon, the Jaguar DS420 was treated to a larger limousine body. The result gave rise to the only model ever made by Jaguar solely under the Daimler name: the Daimler DS420. The body was different in style, stretched out in length and height, and designed for an elite market. Queen Elizabeth II still uses such a car regularly for special occasions.

In 1968, Jaguar replaced all of its saloons with the XJ, which had a more modern look. In 1972, the XJ benefited from the installation of a V12 and was made into an even more luxurious car called the Daimler Double Six. Incidentally, it was this Daimler car that would last across the 1970s and 1980s until the XJ40 V12 was launched in 1993. The XJ (X308) took over until it was replaced with the Daimler Super V6, followed by the Daimler Super Eight in 2005.

ABOVE
Daimlers were sold alongside Jaguar XJs as premier versions.

RIGHT
The interior of the DS420 was designed to accommodate the security personnel of world leaders and other people of great importance.

Although Ford owned Jaguar (and therefore the Daimler brand) for many years from 1990, and didn't hesitate to develop top-of-the-range cars, the American company would not have profited from the Daimler brand. In the end, the Daimler brand was nothing but the icing on the cake. Once Tata Motors bought Jaguar and Land Rover, the Indian manufacturer also became the owner of Daimler.

Throughout the development of all these XJ models under Daimler, Jaguar always maintained its focus on high-quality parts, both for the exterior, which was generally outfitted with chrome, and for the passenger compartments, where high-quality panelling was generously used, and where the back-seat ambience was generally reminiscent of business class.

Daimler DS420
Queen Elizabeth II still uses her Daimler DS420.

Daimler Double Six, 1993

DISPLACEMENT: V12, 5,343cc; **MAX POWER:** 318bhp, **TORQUE:** 34lb ft; rear-wheel drive; four-speed automatic gearbox; **WEIGHT:** 1,760kg (3,880lb).

Jaguar 420

1966

Transition

OPPOSITE
The curves of the 420
were reminiscent of the
older saloons, like the
S-type, but its radiator
design would carry over
to the XJ.

In the mid-1960s, the Jaguar marque – perhaps it would be more accurate to say the Jaguar Group, which owned Daimler – was in superb shape. Exports to the United States accounted for half of production, and the brand's big saloons had managed to raise themselves to Rolls-Royce levels of comfort and prestige, at much more accessible prices. There wasn't a cloud on the horizon. Sir William Lyons, however, was not a man to rest on his laurels. To him, it was essential to improve his range of cars still further. The Jaguar 420 illustrates this wish. Launched in 1966, at the same time as its Daimler Sovereign equivalent, it incorporated the characteristics of the S-type. Lyons knew that the S-type's design was not universally popular, and wanted to rectify this with the 420. The four headlights in a line foreshadowed the future star

saloon of the 1970s, the XJ6, and thus the 420 can be seen as a transitional model. However, the rear of the 420 remained close to that of the S-type.

The car was fitted with the XK 4.2-litre engine, capable of 245bhp – the minimum needed to propel the flagship saloon's 1,650kg (3,638lb) bulk. It also ushered in a new BorgWarner Model 8 automatic gearbox and a new hydraulic braking system. Above all, it benefited from the E-type's rear suspension, with its independently sprung wheels.

From 1967, sales of the Jaguar 420 and Daimler Sovereign confirmed that Lyons had been correct in his action. The Jaguar 420 prefigured the XJ6, which replaced it in 1968. As for the Daimler, it continued in production until 1969, even though a Daimler DS420 had been launched the previous year.

Jaguar 420, 1966

DISPLACEMENT: inline six-cylinder, 4,235cc; **MAX POWER:** 245bhp; **TORQUE:** 283lb ft; naturally aspirated; rear-wheel drive; four-speed manual gearbox or automatic; **WEIGHT:** 1,650kg (3,638lb).

Daimler DS420
1968

Royal

OPPOSITE
The DS420 was hand-built at the Vanden Plas plant, which BMC owned along with Jaguar and Daimler.

The DS420 may be the most important car that Jaguar made in the late 1960s. It evolved from the S-type, the 420G, which was barely distinguishable from the Mark X, and the Daimler DS420. By 1968, Jaguar had owned Daimler for eight years, and the company felt it was high time to update the aging DR450 luxury limousine, the last car designed by Daimler before it was bought by Jaguar.

The DS420 – unveiled in June 1968 and so named because it was built on the chassis of the 420G but lengthened by about 50cm (20in) – was a done deal. Its designers had thought big: it had eight seats and was 6½ft (2m) wide and more than 16½ft (5m) long. It was the 20th century embodiment of a royal coach and was the largest unitary body vehicle in the world. At that point it

would have seemed obvious to install a Daimler V8, as Jaguar had done with the Daimler 250 V8. But Jaguar abandoned this idea in favour of rationalization, and the XK engine, whose assembly lines had long been established, powered nearly all Jaguar cars at the time. The DS420 received the six-cylinder engine in 4.2-litre form. A V12 was later tested in secret, but the weak sales of this imposing limousine didn't allow for recouping the cost of this extra version.

The size and luxuriousness of the DS420 clearly made it an excellent choice as a royal car. Queen Elizabeth II owned five of them. The Danish and Swedish royal families were equally fond of it, as was the Prince of Luxembourg. The DS420 enjoyed a long career that ended in 1992. It was the last car to run on the XK engine.

Daimler DS420, 1968

DISPLACEMENT: inline six-cylinder, 4,235cc; **MAX POWER:** 245bhp; **TORQUE:** 283lb ft; naturally aspired; rear-wheel drive; automatic gearbox; **WEIGHT:** 2,150kg (4,740lb).

Daimler 2.5-litre V8/V8 250

1962-1967

A happy union

The history of Daimler, as we've seen, was a tumultuous one. In 1950, Norah Docker took over the board of directors, which had previously been run by BSA (at the time, a small conglomerate of motorcycle brands). Her escapades and lavish spending quickly bore a hole in the company finances, which were not in good shape. Jaguar ended up purchasing Daimler in 1960 for £3.4m, along with the Radford plant. According to Sir William Lyons, this was the real target of the purchase, as Jaguar's plant at Browns Lane could no longer be expanded. Upon completion of the acquisition, the Jaguar-Daimler Group employed about 8,000 workers.

While it was the Daimler plant, rather than the cars themselves, that had aroused Lyons' interest, he was more than happy to get the company's V8 series. In 1959, Jaguar had just unveiled the pretty Mark II, complete with XK engine. Before too long, engineers came up with the idea of outfitting the Mark II with the V8, which, surprisingly, was about 50kg (110lb) lighter than the six-cylinder XK. Doing so required a few adjustments: the crankcase had to be redesigned so that it could be anchored on

the front axle of the Mark II, new exhaust manifolds needed to be designed to fit into the engine compartment, and the water pump and radiator fan had to be moved. The car was ready in 1962. At first glance, the Daimler 2.5-litre V8 could have easily passed for a Jaguar Mark II, were it not for the Daimler emblem.

The 2.5-litre V8 was the first Daimler released under the aegis of Jaguar, and was a marriage of the finest qualities of the two English carmakers.

Daimlers, little by little, were turning into better-equipped Jaguars. Although the V8 engine lacked significant horsepower at only 140bhp, it turned out to be extremely pleasant and smooth. This made it even more popular, with the middle classes that drove the Mark II, than the XK engine. In 1964, its automatic transmission was replaced with an updated version of the initial BorgWarner model. The following year, transmission ratios were revised to lessen the V8's consumption at cruising speed. Finally, a few manual transmission models were manufactured in 1967 for export.

At the end of 1967, the 2.5-litre V8 became the V8 250, following in Jaguar's footsteps – the Mark II had

ABOVE
The Daimler's 140bhp belied the smoothness of its engine, which, by the end of the 1960s, was on its last legs.

RIGHT
Daimler's V8 was designed for Edward Turner, the longstanding British head of the Triumph Motorcycle Company.

just given way to the 240 and then the 340. Daimler carried on in this vein while maintaining its high-quality mechanics and replacing the old dynamo (generator) with an alternator. It added a few interior details, including a heated rear windscreen and power steering, but the V8 250 remained less well-equipped than the Jaguar 340, which created confusion regarding Daimler's position within the "Jaguar Group". Nevertheless, Daimlers met with a certain degree of success and were popular in the United States. A total of more than 17,000 models of the 2.5-litre V8 and V8 250 were sold between 1962 and 1969. Production halted when the new XJ arrived and replaced all of Jaguar's and Daimler's 1960s saloons (240, 340, 420 and so on). The Daimler Sovereign was unveiled in 1969. This was a better-equipped Jaguar XJ6, now outfitted with a XK engine.

Daimler 2.5-litre V8/V8 250

The Daimler V8 was popular with the upper-middle class of the time.

Daimler 2.5-litre V8, 1962

DISPLACEMENT: V8, 2,548cc; **MAX POWER:** 140bhp; **TORQUE:** 155lb ft; naturally aspirated; rear-wheel drive; four-speed manual or automatic gearbox; **WEIGHT:** 1,450kg (3,197lb).

XJ6
1968

Timeless

OPPOSITE

The XJ6 was launched in 1968 and straight away set new standards for ride comfort and refinement. It continued through three generations until supplanted by the XJ40 models in 1986.

The XJ series made its mark on the history of the motorcar. Originally, the XJ's destiny was tied to that of the E-type, as if all modern Jaguars were descended from it. Sir William Lyons had expressed a desire for a saloon based on the coupé, which had been launched in 1961, or at least a more comfortable version of the "small" E-type. This gave rise to an initial concept car, dubbed the XJ4. Other versions, some far removed from this first design, were also built, but there was considerable debate among the engineers involved. Twenty of them put enormous effort into designing the first XJ series, under the leadership of William Heynes. The model finally took shape in 1966. Its rounded lines were inspired by the Mark 2, but the XJ models were lower and more elongated, as modern style demanded. Roadholding was high on the list of criteria, and the mechanical components would be derived from the XK model line.

The Jaguar XJ6 ("X" standing for "Xperimental", "J" for "Jaguar", and "6" for the number of cylinders) was finally unveiled in 1968, at the Paris Motor Show. It came with two six-cylinder engines – a 2.8-litre and a 4.2-litre – and a manual or automatic gearbox. Its chassis was based on a steel load-bearing shell, and an innovative structure featuring progressive deformation. A distinctive feature of the XJ was its two fuel tanks, with filler caps either side of the boot. Production was difficult at first, because of frequent labour unrest during the late 1960s at Pressed Steel Fisher, Jaguar's historical supplier of bodywork panels. The success of the first Jaguar XJ6s (known simply as the "XJ" in the US) was down to the saloon's roadholding, comfort and braking. The 4.2-litre automatic was the most sought-after at the time.

The XJ was also launched under the Daimler brand in 1969 in the form of the Sovereign, distinguished by a radiator grille with a ribbed upper part and an even more luxurious interior. In July 1972, the Jaguar XJ12 (Double Six in its Daimler version), featuring the 5.3-litre V12 engine from the E-type S3, was added to the range alongside the XJ6. Its 253bhp earned it the honorary title of the world's fastest saloon car, with a top speed of around 140mph. Two wheelbases were available, the longer one like that of a small limousine.

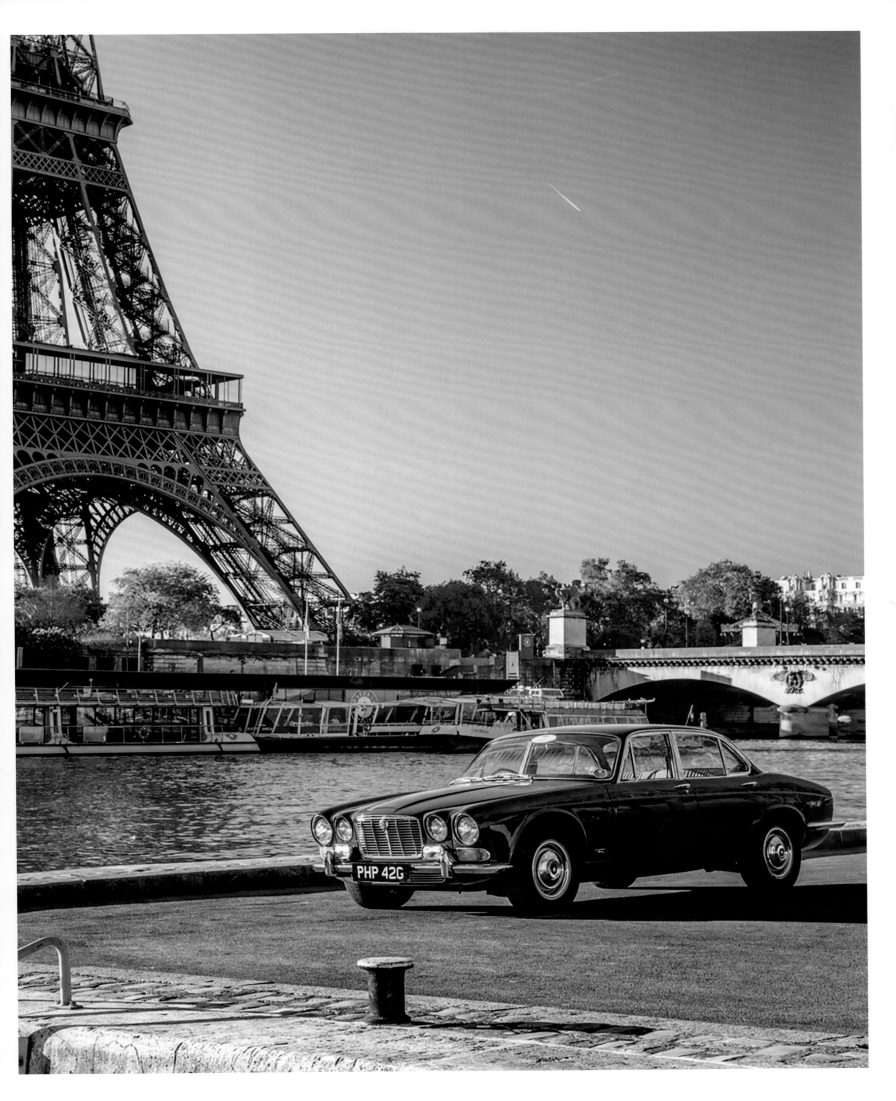

XJ6

As early as 1968, the Jaguar XJ6's British charm allowed it to rival the most beautiful saloons in Europe.

OPPOSITE, TOP
The first XJ6 was available in two versions: one with a 2.8-litre inline six-cylinder, and the other with the same engine structure, but with a 4.2-litre engine.

OPPOSITE, BOTTOM
The Series 1, with its gleaming chromes, exuded old-fashioned charm. Jaguar produced more 4.2-litre models than 2.8-litre ones.

ABOVE
The 4.2-litre model remained at the top of the line until 1972, the year the XJ12 was released. The XJ12's 5.3-litre V12 engine was borrowed from the E-type Series 3.

ABOVE
The XJ6 saloon became available in XJ6, and XJ12 coupé versions in 1974. These were pulled from the catalogue in 1978, after underwhelming sales.

RIGHT
The XJ6 Landaulet, which was fully convertible, was especially well-suited to prestigious ceremonies, such as those of the British royal family.

The following year the XJ underwent its first updating. The 2.8-litre engine was replaced by a 3.4-litre six-cylinder unit, which produced 163bhp. The V12 was fitted with Bosch fuel injection. This second version of the XJ (Series II) continued in production until 1979, by which time 91,000 had been sold to satisfied customers the world over. A coupé, the XJC, made a brief appearance between 1975 and 1978. Although very handsome, it fell victim to the economic troubles afflicting both Europe and the US.

Finally, the Series III took over in 1980. It had been redesigned by the Italian company Pininfarina and was recognizable by its rubber bumpers and flush door handles. Three engines were offered: a 5.3-litre V12, a 4.2-litre straight-six and a 3.4-litre straight-six. The Sovereign trim level now bore the Jaguar name rather than Daimler.

It cannot be said that the XJ has died out, even though today's version is a far cry from the first series. A record lifespan for a saloon car!

XJ6

Upon its release in 1972, the Jaguar XJ12 was the only saloon equipped with a V12.

Jaguar XJ6, 1968

DISPLACEMENT: inline six-cylinder, 2,792cc; MAX POWER: 180bhp; TORQUE: 182lb ft; naturally aspirated; rear-wheel drive; four-speed manual gearbox or three-speed automatic; WEIGHT: 1,450kg (3,197lb).

The most reliable XK engine was the 3.8-litre
used in the XK150 or the E-type.

The six-cylinder automaker

| 1948 |

While the Jaguar name is now more commonly associated with 12-cylinder engines, the inline six-cylinder remains historically the carmaker's most charming and significant: the first SS cars were equipped with the inline six produced by Standard. These were later improved upon by Jaguar engineers, especially by Harry Weslake, starting in 1934.

It made sense for the first Jaguar engine, the XK, to revive this inline six-cylinder in 1948. It involved a cast-iron block with an 83mm (3¼in) bore and a 106mm (4¼in) stroke. The aluminium cylinder head accommodated two camshafts. The basic version's horsepower measured 160bhp. It was first installed in the Jaguar XK120, but its various iterations powered the XK140, XK150, Mark I, Mark II, Mark VII, Mark VIII, until the XJ6 in the 1980s, as well as the prestigious C- and D-types. Few engines have experienced such a long lifespan.

The temptation of using a V12 loomed large early on in the history of Jaguar, ever since 1950, especially for racing. The first car to really incorporate the Jaguar V12 engine was the XJ13, of which only one was ever made. The V12 wasn't used again in a Jaguar until the E-type Series 3 came out in 1971.

ABOVE
The XK engine (the XK120 is shown above) enjoyed an extremely long career. It started in 1948 with the XK120, and production ended in 1992 along with that of the Daimler DS420.

XJ12
1972

Fast feline

The inline six-cylinder engine that Sir William Lyons developed at the end of the 1940s was revolutionary. When the very first XJ saw the light of day in 1968, it was considered the most beautiful saloon in the world. But that little bit extra – a V12 engine – that would allow Lyons to measure himself against the Italians from Maranello and Sant'Agata was nevertheless missing. When the V12 engine was introduced with the E-type Series 3 in 1971, it was clear that to install it in the XJ would create one of the most powerful saloons in the world, and would cement Jaguar's position of excellence.

In 1972, when Lyons retired (although he retained a certain amount of power over decision-making until his death in 1985), the XJ12 and its twin sister the Daimler Double Six went on sale. What set these two apart was essentially the higher level of trim on the Daimler than on the XJ base model. However,

once seated in the XJ12, the driver was totally charmed by the dashboard's very vertical design and, of course, by the luxuriousness of the materials, which, right through to the XJ12 Series 3, had always been of the highest quality.

In 1972, the Jaguar XJ12's 5.3-litre V12 produced 250bhp, a considerable achievement for the time. However, its German competitors would bring out their own V12 engines (BMW in 1987, Mercedes in 1991), which were more powerful, and at the end of the 1980s, 250bhp was no longer an exceptional power output. What surprised XJ12 drivers was the impressive torque available from 3,500rpm, and the automatic gearbox, which offered a lot of driving pleasure. Although the V12's fuel consumption was too high when it was launched, it would be progressively reduced with each successive generation.

OPPOSITE
In 1972, the XJ12 was one of the fastest saloons in the world.

Jaguar XJ12, 1972

DISPLACEMENT: V12, 5,343cc; **MAX POWER:** 250bhp; **TORQUE:** 301lb ft; naturally aspirated; rear-wheel drive; three-speed automatic gearbox; **WEIGHT:** 1,760kg (3,880lb).

1973

Beautiful, but ephemeral

From 1968, the XJ saloon was one of the most beautiful cars on the market. Nevertheless, Jaguar launched the Series 2 as early as 1973. However, the launch of a coupé version after that – with a shortened platform – perhaps came a little late. Only two years after the XJ coupé, in 1975, Jaguar launched the coupé XJS, a car aimed at pretty much the same clientele – the result of an internal conflict of the sort that occurred frequently at the time. In hindsight, it would doubtless have been wiser to launch this XJ coupé earlier, in 1968.

The fact remains that the XJC retained the generous, rounded lines of the saloon. More compact, being 4in (10cm) shorter, the coupé possessed all the elegance and refined lines for which the XJ was famous. This was true of the interior as well, which had the same dashboard and offered the same level of refinement as that of the saloon. Only the room for the rear seats was slightly reduced, but the car's interior space was perfectly designed for four people.

Even though the oil crisis was raging, under the bonnet there was a 4.2-litre inline six-cylinder engine (XJ 4.2C) or the all-new 5.3-litre V12 (XJ 5.3C) – enough to offer excellent road performance with very comfortable suspension. Only 13 cars were built in 1973, and the XJC would never be sold in large numbers during its short life of barely four years – a total of almost 10,500 XJC cars were sold worldwide.

OPPOSITE
Although the XJC adopted the look and shape of the XJ saloon, it remained 10cm (4in) shorter.

Jaguar XJ 4.2 C, 1973

DISPLACEMENT: inline six-cylinder, 4,235cc; **MAX POWER:** 180bhp, **TORQUE:** 232lb ft; naturally aspirated; rear-wheel drive; three-speed automatic gearbox; **WEIGHT:** 1,764kg (3,889lb).

The XJC V12, enhanced to produce 560bhp, suffered from rather spotty reliability.

A painful racing result

| 1976 |

The late 1960s and early 1970s were not an ideal era for racing innovations. In 1966, Jaguar was acquired by BMC, which became BLMC two years later (see pages 60–63), making the time unsuitable for the use of "imagination". Some E-types were still involved in various tests, but this was not public knowledge. Nevertheless, one man tried to convince Jaguar executives of the importance of racing in preserving Jaguar's image. Racer and engineer Ralph Broad ended up getting what he wanted. Two XJC 5.3-litre engines were put together in his Broadspeed workshops for participation in the 1976 European Touring Car Championship. While a series of wins in the qualifiers won the cars recognition, the V12's unreliability let them down in the actual race: 14 breakdowns out of 17 starts! The result Broad had been hoping for – the promotion of the brand – ended up being a curse rather than a blessing.

Later, the XJ-S met with much better results in Europe and the United States, thanks to Tom Walkinshaw's TWR team, which was officially supported by Jaguar.

ABOVE AND RIGHT
Broadspeed's XJC was reprised with the same body and a 295bhp engine for the famous TV series, *The Avengers*.

XJ-S

1975

A hard act to follow

The 1970s were a difficult time for Britain. Industry was faltering, and BMC, which had taken over Jaguar in 1966, did not escape the slump. Although Jaguar were enjoying success in the American market, the sourcing of raw material and unrest among the workforce made production difficult. Other British brands were experiencing the same problems, especially the motorcycle industry (Triumph, Norton and BSA). And this was without even taking account of the 1973 oil crisis.

A new nationalized group, BLMC, was formed in 1968, bringing together British Motor Holdings and Leyland Motor Corporation. Austin, Leyland, Morris, Triumph, Rover and Jaguar were now under the same banner.

As one restructuring followed another, Jaguar was losing its independence and had to yield to the rationalization measures implemented by the Group. Production of the E-type ended in 1975, and the XJC coupés never enjoyed success. A replacement for the flamboyant line of sporty Jaguar grand tourers was needed.

William Heynes still believed, at the end of the 1960s, in the possibility of a coupé based on the XJ platform. He designed several prototypes, one of which was built in 1969. The look of the coupé had been the subject of various studies entrusted to several designers, but the design by Malcolm Sayer, which retained the now iconic long bonnet, found favour. Sayer tragically died in 1970, during the development of the future XJ-S, and was replaced by Doug Thorpe. Thorpe had produced an earlier design, but this was rejected by management and Sir William Lyons (the latter still had influence over decisions, even though he was by now retired).

The mechanical components of the XJ-S were based on the E-type's V12 engine. The XJ-S ("S" for "Special") was unveiled in September 1975 in London. It featured only this engine, an imposing 5.3-litre V12 producing 285bhp, above all as a way of emphasizing the top-of-the-range, upmarket status of the E-type's replacement. Its price followed suit – initially in line with that of the last E-type, it then increased to double that sum! Fuel consumption was equally hefty – the V12 was thirsty, despite its fuel injection, and had to propel a car weighing more than 1.6 tonnes.

OPPOSITE
When the XJ-S first came out it only had one engine: the enormous V12.

XJ-S

Despite its size, the XJ-S took part in many international competitions.

OPPOSITE, TOP
Car tuners produced
some impressive
versions of the XJ-S in
the late 1980s, including
this 500bhp XJ-S 7.

OPPOSITE, BOTTOM
The specifications
of the XJ-S could
compete with those
of any Porsche,
while maintaining an
exemplary speed.

ABOVE
Little by little, the interior
of the XJ-S caught up
with its luxury rivals:
the early cars' wood
interiors were replaced
with plastic.

ABOVE
The four-grille lights set
American models apart.

RIGHT
The E-type made a name
for the Jaguar V12, but the
XJ-S gave it a new life. The
image opposite shows two
XJS models from the 1990s:
a coupé and a convertible.

The public was not thrilled by the XJ-S in 1975. The legacy of the E-type was an even heavier burden than the XJ-S's steel and aluminium. The car lacked sportiness, and its more conventional design suffered by comparison with the aggressive Ferraris and Lamborghinis. Likewise, the plastic interior fittings made people long for the burr walnut of past Jaguars. The transition to the modern era for such an authentic marque was not an easy one. Only its engine's extreme smoothness found favour with those who test drove it. TV series such as *The Saint*

and *The Avengers* improved the XJ-S's image, but not enough to bring commercial success.

The early 1980s saw an update to the XJ-S. Its V12 was reworked in 1981, gaining some 30bhp, and in 1983 a more modest 3.6-litre, six-cylinder version was introduced to the Jaguar coupé range. There was a final update in 1991: the six-cylinder engine's displacement was increased to 4 litres. The following year, the V12's was increased to 6 litres.

The XJ-S ended production in 1996; more than 110,000 were built over 20 years.

XJ-S

The XJ-S had big boots to fill when it replaced the celebrated E-type.

Jaguar XJ-S, 1975

DISPLACEMENT: V12, 5,343cc; MAX POWER: 285bhp; TORQUE: 294lb ft; naturally aspirated; rear-wheel drive; five-speed manual gearbox or automatic; WEIGHT: 1,692kg (3,730lb).

XJ Series III
1979

Persistence

The last facelift the XJ6 underwent was in 1979, not long before the arrival of its replacement, the XJ40 series. However, the XJ12 model's lifespan extended right up to 1993. From 1974, the engineer Geoffrey Robinson had suggested a reworking of the XJ6, focusing the project on build quality. But BLMC's management was trying to cut costs in every way possible, rather than investing. Nevertheless, starting in 1976, research and development were undertaken with the aim of modernizing the marque's flagship saloon and allowing it to continue to compete with German brands, particularly Mercedes.

To avoid the need for colossal investment (£7m, no less), the XJ Series III would not differ very markedly from the Series II. The Italian designer Sergio Pininfarina was entrusted with the task. He tried to improve the XJ without making changes that would disrupt the production lines. His redesign was subtle. It consisted chiefly of a finer radiator grille, a higher roofline and an increased window area, as well as flush door handles and bumpers with integrated indicators. The small, cathedral-shaped tail-lights gave way to a new,

more modern design, and the roof panel was flatter. The two filler caps were retained for the twin fuel tanks. Inside, the seats were more comfortable, with adjustable lumbar support. New carpeting, better-arranged instrumentation and a higher standard of finish completed these minor innovations.

On the mechanical side, the only change was to the six-cylinder, 4.2-litre engine. This now featured fuel injection, which had become necessary to comply with anti-pollution regulations. This reduced fuel consumption, improved performance and enabled the engine to produce 205bhp. The six-cylinder 3.4-litre version, which retained its carburettors, was for this reason not exported to the United States, where regulations were stricter. The V12, by contrast, had been given fuel injection in 1975, but was improved in 1980 with a higher compression ratio and Lucas fuel injection.

During the 1970s and early 1980s, the only other marques that made V12 engines were Ferrari and Lamborghini. Jaguar's V12 differed from these in its smoothness and broad power band, which suited its General Motors automatic gearbox. It nevertheless

OPPOSITE
Keeping the XJ Series III in production proved to be particularly expensive for Jaguar.

XJ Series III

In the early 1980s, the Jaguar XJ12 was the fastest saloon in the world.

OPPOSITE, TOP
The XJ Series III was a lounge on wheels. Today, it's an interesting collector's piece, as its parts can easily be found in Great Britain.

OPPOSITE, BOTTOM
The Series III was modernized by the Italian designer Sergio Pininfarina. The sizes of the windows were increased.

ABOVE
For its fiftieth anniversary, a very special XJ6 was displayed at the 2018 Geneva Motor Show – that of Nicko McBrain, Iron Maiden's drummer.

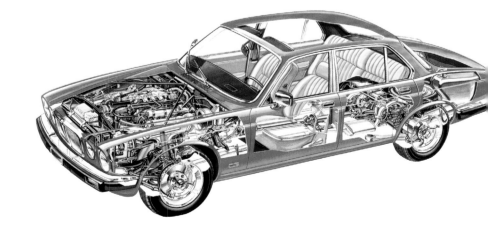

ABOVE
The XJ Series III enjoyed a long career. It developed alongside anti-pollution standards and with the demands of its various target markets.

RIGHT
A new Rover five-speed manual gearbox was unveiled with the release of the Series III.

allowed the big saloon to reach a top speed of almost 150mph.

In 1980, John Egan, who had just become head of Jaguar, initially wanted to design a new model quickly. However, faced with the scale of the task, he changed his mind. Nevertheless, the XJ40 project was launched in 1986 and, paradoxically, the XJ Series III was given a boost. In 1981, Jaguar XJ12 and Daimler Double Six benefited from new V12 engines. These featured new pistons and Fireball cylinder heads, but slightly less power as a trade-off for increased torque. These new V12 engines were

badged HE (High Efficiency). In 1984, the Daimler Sovereign was replaced by the Jaguar Sovereign, and the Daimler Double Six Vanden Plas by the luxurious Jaguar Vanden Plas HE. Sales of the XJ had never been so healthy.

The six-cylinder XJ models were discontinued in 1987, to be replaced by the XJ40, but the XJ12 continued its career until 1992, when it was replaced by the XJ81, the V12 version of the XJ40.

From its launch in 1968, about 318,000 XJ cars were built. The Series III alone accounted for 132,952 of these; only 10,500 were XJ12 models.

XJ Series III
Anti-pollution standards gradually robbed the XJ12 of its power.

Jaguar XJ Series III, 1979

DISPLACEMENT: V12, 5,343cc; **MAX POWER:** 287bhp; **TORQUE:** 294lb ft; naturally aspirated; rear-wheel drive; automatic gearbox; **WEIGHT:** 1,900kg (4,189lb).

HISTORY

A long, hard road

1974 > 1986

In 1974, BLMC started to chalk up its first losses. Harold Wilson, then Britain's prime minister, granted the conglomerate a loan on condition that it carried out a complete audit. The Ryder Report, submitted on 26 March, proposed creating unity between the production sites of the various British Leyland brands (Jaguar, Land Rover, Rover, Mini, Austin, Morris, MG, Triumph, Daimler and so on). The aim was to streamline and, above all, avoid the duplication of models across the different brands.

Rationalization needed

The need to share some parts in order to cut production costs – as Volkswagen and Porsche were already doing – had become vital for BLMC. The only drawback for Jaguar was the loss of total independence, which its founder, Sir William Lyons, then in a position of "pre-retirement", had put in place and promised to all employees.

In fact, the report demonstrated that Jaguar had initially negotiated better purchase prices with suppliers than the BLMC Group itself, and so it was therefore logical that Lyons should disagree with the report's conclusions. Of course, Lyons had many allies within the company. Jaguar's boss, Geoffrey Robinson, was also fiercely opposed to the Ryder

Geoffrey Robinson led Jaguar for two years, between 1973 and 1975.

Report. As a result, he began construction of a new paint-shop, when he knew perfectly well that British Leyland was going to put Triumph's at his disposal. Robinson decided to resign from Jaguar in May 1975. After his departure, the paint-shop did not, in the end, see the light of day. In solidarity with Robinson, Jaguar's employees decided to go on strike in protest, and to demand that he stay at the company. However, Robinson had other, more political ambitions within the Labour government.

At the same time, Jaguar once again fitted its XJ models with the 3.4-litre inline six-cylinder engine, in order to offer customers a unit that was simpler to maintain. The 4.2-litre engine was then fitted to the XJ Vanden Plas, while the 5.3-litre V12 was improved with the addition of electronic fuel injection.

Two competing coupés

During this period, Jaguar also began large-scale production of the XJ coupé (XJ6 C), unveiled at the Luxembourg Motor Show in 1973. This superb coupé soon turned heads and enjoyed great success – even on the small screen, where an XJ12 C appeared in the series *The Avengers*. At the time, the XJ coupé met with the unanimous

John Egan, here seen surrounded by his management committee, visited a number of competing plants before developing the ideal production system for Jaguar.

Production streamlining at Jaguar was a headache until the mid-1980s and beyond; at least until Ford acquired the company in 1990.

All Jaguars produced between 1951 and 1998 were made at Browns Lane, which until recently hosted the Jaguar Daimler Heritage Trust, a tribute to the brand.

approval of the specialist motoring press because of its quietness and comfort, and the effectiveness of its six-cylinder engine and chassis. But Jaguar urgently needed to rationalize its production sites. The XJC alone required a production line, and it was necessary to reduce the number of versions of the XJ. Production of the coupé was therefore stopped in 1977, as was that of the Daimler Sovereign version of the XJ. Jaguar also tried to develop the XJ coupé in motorsport. Indeed, it was Ralph Broad who had floated the idea of the manufacturer returning to competition a few years earlier. But it was no use. The XJC never really excelled on European racetracks.

In the meantime, the Coventry company launched another upmarket coupé with a much more innovative style: the XJ-S. This coupé had been conceived during the 1960s through a whole series of prototypes. The 1969 prototype, developed by Lyons and Malcolm Sayer, who was then in charge of design, featured flat-topped arches at the rear, rectangular headlights, which were highly unusual for the marque (and incidentally needed to be made to measure by the French company Cibié), and flattened, slightly curved lines. As well as providing a successor to the E-type, the XJ-S coupé's role was also to compete with a certain Ford Thunderbird in the United States. But the pervading crisis and the rise in the cost of oil hardly helped the XJ-S coupé. Sales began to fall in 1976, only a year after its launch, dropping to a miserable 1,000 units for the year 1980. It must be said that this must-have car boasted a 5.3-litre V12, whose fuel consumption was a bit high at the time of an oil crisis.

In the early 1980s, Jaguar produced a more fuel-efficient V12, the HE (High Efficiency) in response. The convertible version of the XJ-S, built by Lynx, revitalized sales somewhat when it was launched in 1983. Meanwhile, British Leyland continued to founder, with huge losses, taking Jaguar with it. Faced with what they saw as inaction on the part of management, employees and workers embarked on a series of strikes. The quality and, above all, the reliability of the cars deteriorated rapidly as

a result. In the late 1970s, it was not unusual for the windscreen wipers on an XJ Double Six to fail in torrential rain. Numerous other failings were reported by customers, such as problems with leaking bodywork and electrical failures. It was an extremely difficult time, during which Jaguar's image as regards reliability was greatly damaged. A noble marque had hit rock bottom. But the XJ Series III then came on the market, and allowed the company to recover a little of its verve. Even though it echoed the design of its predecessor, this big saloon was completely innovative in a number of respects.

Indomitable defenders

At the same time, another department of the manufacturer was working on a completely new generation of the XJ, codenamed XJ40. The war being waged between Jaguar's management and that of BLMC led the former to take decisions that went as far as the size of the XJ40's engine compartment. In concrete terms, it was impossible to fit Rover's big V8 into it. British Leyland was thus unable to share this bulky "mass-market" engine with an upmarket marque such as Jaguar. This internal conflict went so far that certain essential developments were delayed and even postponed. This was the case with the system for preventing the wheels from locking up when braking, already known as ABS (anti-lock braking system), which was eventually launched by German competitors.

BLMC continued to experience big losses – despite a £1 billion loan approved by Margaret Thatcher. In 1980, John Egan, an ardent defender of Jaguar, was appointed head of the company. Practically minded, he did not hesitate to seek advice from Lyons, sent managers to Germany and Japan to study best practice in the car industry – specifically the famous "quality circles" – and improved relations between management and the workforce. All these decisions transformed the company, which, in just a few years, increased in value, especially after privatization in 1984. It was enough to arouse the interest of other big car manufacturing groups…

A 1980 marketing campaign highlighted Jaguar's newfound independence after breaking off from the big conglomerates.

1975
Jaguar launched the XJ-S, aiming to compete with the Ford Thunderbird in the United States.

In April 1980, workers with the Transport and General Workers' Union (TGWU) expressed their dissatisfaction with Browns Lane.

John Egan, left, and Sir William Lyons, right, had a long discussion about management at the start of the 1980s.

Browns Lane was home to the model for the XJ-S prototype. The first prototype was created in 1969.

XJ40

1986

A vital model

Jaguar had profound changes in mind for the XJ in the early 1970s, and embarked on a project named XJ40. This codename would be kept as the model name of the fourth-generation XJ. The aim was to replace the XJ6 and restore some of Jaguar's dynamism. British Leyland, which had to endure the effects of the oil crisis, put back the project, which involved a different design, several times. Finally, in 1981, it gave it the green light. After years in development and numerous postponements, the XJ40 was launched in 1986.

The XJ40 became vitally important to Jaguar's future. The XJ Series III and XJ-S were dated, and there was also the issue of reliability. The XJ40 therefore represented Jaguar's resurgence. It was based on a new technical platform, with new engines and drivetrains, and its assembly required fewer body panels than the Series III. Although the overall shape of the XJ was retained, the front featured new rectangular headlights, which went down rather badly with the marque's enthusiasts. As for the interior, the XJ40 came in three versions: the basic XJ6 and the more lavishly furnished Sovereign and Daimler. The Sovereign model

was generously equipped and had a luxurious interior featuring climate control, ABS, SLS (self-levelling suspension) and six loudspeakers as standard. The more "business orientated" Daimler model, with its two separate rear seats and aircraft-style tables in burr walnut, had a host of other finishing touches such as the small lights built into the front headrests, and reading lamps mounted behind the headrests at the rear. Everything was encased in chrome and high-quality leather, which has tended to remain in exceptionally good condition decades later.

More modern cars, like the XJ40, also needed to be reliable with engines that were beyond reproach. Accordingly, Jaguar introduced a completely new range of inline six-cylinder engines, called the AJ6. The entry-level 2.9-litre engine, which produced 165bhp, was very limiting for such a saloon, and was replaced by a 3.2-litre with 200bhp. But the 3.6-litre engine, producing 221bhp, and the 4-litre unit with 223bhp that replaced it in 1989 were undeniably engines worth having, thanks to their ease of driving and their reliability. The 3.2-litre engine also featured (in supercharged form) in the Aston Martin DB7 from

XJ40

The XJ40 was the last car to be designed under the direction of Sir William Lyons.

OPPOSITE, TOP
Some XJ40 models came with round headlights. These were mostly used on base models, such as the XJ6 seen here.

OPPOSITE, BOTTOM
The XJ40 experimented with new interior features, such as an onboard computer by the steering wheel.

ABOVE
The back seat of the Daimler was extremely comfortable and acted as an exceptional workspace.

ABOVE
The XJ40 inaugurated a completely new range of inline six-cylinder engine. The base model's 2.9-litre engine was later replaced by a 3.2-litre 203bhp engine.

RIGHT
All Sovereign models were equipped with an ABS and an SLS.

1994 to 1999. Although also available with a five-speed manual gearbox, the XJ40 was nevertheless to be preferred with the various versions of the ZF four-speed automatic gearbox.

The XJR was also the sportiest model. To start with, it featured the 3.6-litre six-cylinder engine, although this was quickly replaced by a 4-litre unit producing 248bhp. Its distinctive features were wider-diameter wheels and, above all, its black (rather than chrome) radiator grille. From 1992, the 4-litre Daimler was one of the most accomplished models, not only because of its exceptional engine but also its even more comprehensive equipment, which included a limited-slip differential, a "sport" mode for the automatic gearbox, cruise control, heated front seats, electric sunroof and the now de rigueur six-disc CD changer located in the boot. It could reach 62mph in 8.1 seconds and cruise at almost 140mph with a high level of comfort.

XJ40

In total, more than 208,000 XJ40s were produced.

Jaguar XJ40, 1986

DISPLACEMENT: inline 6-cylinder, 3,590cc; **MAX POWER:** 221bhp; **TORQUE:** 248lb ft; rear-wheel drive; four-speed automatic gearbox; **WEIGHT:** 1,770kg (3,902lb).

Daimler
Double Six
1993

The essential saloon

OPPOSITE

With its 318bhp V12, the Daimler Double Six was one of the greatest, fastest and most comfortable saloons of 1993.

Many people wondered, at the launch of the XJ40, why Jaguar did not offer a V12-engined XJ12 or Daimler Double Six version of the XJ model. Instead, the XJ Series III, which by then was outdated, continued to be available in these luxury versions right up to 1992.

It would appear that the reason was political. When the XJ40 was being designed in the early 1970s, Jaguar engineers – fearing that their counterparts at Rover, which was also controlled by British Leyland at the time, would impose their big V8 engine upon them – deliberately saw to it that only an inline six could be fitted into the engine compartment. It would therefore have been difficult to fit the Jaguar V12 that had been used in the previous generation XJs since 1972.

Nowadays, few people would be tempted by a V12 engine in a technically outdated car with a reputation for unreliability. But in 1993, the engineers reworked the engine. Its displacement was increased to 6 litres and it was combined with a four-speed automatic gearbox. Above all it could – at last – be fitted to the XJ40. The result was a large saloon with 318bhp, which could dispatch the standing kilometre in less than 28 seconds. This did not, for all that, make it a sports car, but rather a saloon for travelling in total comfort. The car's ABS performed better, and the locking differential improved its safety. Aside from these technical improvements, the Daimler Double Six version offered an interior of the utmost refinement – an extremely luxurious ambiance that could unhesitatingly be compared to that found in a Rolls-Royce. This ultimate XJ40s were in production for only two years, and are therefore fairly rare today.

Daimler Double Six, 1993

DISPLACEMENT: V12 5,994cc; **MAX POWER:** 318bhp; **TORQUE:** 342lb ft; rear-wheel drive; four-speed automatic gearbox; **WEIGHT:** 2,050kg (4,519lb).

Although it missed out on the 1990 world title,
the XJR-12 won the Le Mans 24 Hours.

A triumphant return

| 1983 |

In 1983, Jaguar was finally beginning to enjoy renewed success in Europe. In the United States – the world's biggest car market at the time – Jaguar returned to endurance racing to revive sales. Mike Dale, then executive director of Jaguar USA, decided to give Bob Tullius and his racing team at Group 44 the job of building the XJR-5. This prototype distinguished itself in the IMSA GT Championship until 1985.

Meanwhile in Britain, Tom Walkinshaw, the boss of TWR (a team that had won acclaim for its many wins) convinced John Egan, then head of Jaguar, to commit fully to motor racing with the aim of increasing publicity. TWR embarked on designing a new car fitted with a V12 Jaguar engine. The result was the XJR-6, a prototype boasting 650bhp and painstaking aerodynamics work – enough to worry Porsche on the track.

On 5 May 1986, Jaguar returned to winning form in the 1,000 km of Silverstone, with drivers Derek Warwick and Eddie Cheever. The same year, Jaguar came very

RIGHT
This is the cockpit (XJR-9) in which Martin Brundle became the 1988 world champion.

The XJR-8 achieved a double win in 1987, when it bagged world titles for both the manufacturer and the driver.

close to winning the World Sportscar Championship. In 1987, the XJR-8, with an engine displacement of 7 litres, producing 720bhp, won the World Sportscar Championships for both the team and the Brazilian driver Raul Boesel. In 1988, the engine gained a little more horsepower, reaching 750bhp, and the car was renamed the XJR-9. In June, it confirmed its prowess with a victory at the Le Mans 24 Hours. During the race, the trio of Jan Lammers, Johnny Dumfries and Andy Wallace managed to achieve an average speed of 137mph. It was during that season that the Jaguar XJR-9 often got the better of the Porsche 962Cs.

The XJR-9, however, failed to repeat its success in 1989, and Jaguar lost no time moving on, launching the XJR-10 and XJR-11, which featured a turbocharged V6 engine producing 650 and 750bhp. The V12 was put aside, in order to better comply with new regulations and also to lighten the car. During the 1989 and 1990 seasons, Sauber Mercedes made life difficult for the Silk Cut Jaguar team, but the British nevertheless won at Le Mans with the XJR-12. TWR had indeed taken advantage of the change in regulations to embark on the development of a totally new car.

Jaguar won the World Sportscar Championship in 1991 with the XJR-14, powered by its Cosworth V8 engine. However, because of the recession of the early 1990s, Jaguar lacked the means to develop the XJR-14 properly, and the car struggled to compete with the Peugeot 905 Evo, which performed better than ever. The XJR-14 would later be used as the basis for the Mazda MXR-01, because the Japanese manufacturer could no longer use the rotary engine. Indeed, it was Mazda that would represent the Ford Group in endurance racing. In 1993 and 1994, the return of the GT category in endurance racing allowed TWR and Jaguar to enter some XJ220 cars. After 1994, Jaguar did not return to competition until 2000, this time in Formula One.

RIGHT
The XJR-9 V12 produced 750bhp. It brought Jaguar to victory at the Le Mans 24 Hours in 1988.

XJ220

1992

The quickest in the world!

Without a doubt, the XJ220 was one of the most extraordinary Jaguars of all time – yet it had the greatest difficulty being brought into production. In 1984, when Jaguar announced its great return to endurance racing, John Egan, its boss, put together a small team of enthusiasts with the aim of designing an exceptional model derived directly from the technology used in the Jaguar prototypes that competed notably in the Le Mans 24 Hours. In 1988, Jaguar tasted victory once more at Le Mans, 30 years after the XK, and unveiled the XJ220 concept car. This project – which seemed almost crazy at the time – was intended to compete with the small number of supercars already in existence: the Porsche 959 and, of course, the Ferrari F40. Its name was an indication that just 220 were to be built but, because of strong demand from wealthy clients, Jaguar planned on 350 – though this would take time, because production did not begin until 1992.

This enormous coupé looked like nothing that had gone before. Whereas other supercars were complex and bristling with aerodynamic appendages, the XJ220 must have had the most flowing lines in the history of Jaguar. It looked as if it had been sculpted, with each panel of its bodywork designed to slice through the air as efficiently as possible. Its lines also aimed to create downforce and give it aerodynamic stability at very high speed. This extraordinary design was the work of Keith Helfet. The car's dimensions were also out of the ordinary: it was almost 16½ft (5m) long and, most strikingly, 7¼ft (2.22m) wide – while its roof was just 1.1m (3½ft) above the ground! It was truly an unidentified road-going object! And yet, the big cat was right there, in the middle of the radiator grille, incidentally referencing the E-type.

The prototype of the XJ220 could almost take the starting line at the Le Mans 24 Hours. Its cockpit – for it was just that – featured a rev counter (tachometer)

OPPOSITE
With its 542bhp V6 3.5-litre twin-turbo engine, the Jaguar XJ220 was one of the highest-performing supercars of all time.

XJ220

In the early 1990s, the Jaguar XJ220 was the world's fastest and most expensive car.

OPPOSITE, TOP
Released as a concept car in 1988, the XJ220 reached its first customers in 1992.

OPPOSITE, BOTTOM
Despite being very powerful, the V12 Jaguar engine proved too bulky. It was replaced by this twin-turbo V6 engine.

ABOVE
Unlike other supercars, the Jaguar XJ220 had a very smooth profile. The reason: to achieve perfect aerodynamic resistance and improve stability at top speeds.

ABOVE
The XJ220 could reach 62mph in 3.8 seconds and a top speed of 213mph, making it the fastest production car until the McLaren F1's release.

RIGHT
Any unsold XJ220s were bought by TWR to create the TWR220s, lighter and more advanced models which produced 680bhp and competed in the Le Mans 24 Hours in 1993.

with a red line of 7,000rpm and a speedometer that went up to 230mph. Like the 959, but unlike the F40, the rest of the passenger compartment was high-end, with bucket seats offering the perfect position. There was no question of a V12 at the rear – to keep the weight down, Jaguar had fitted a 3.5-litre V6 with twin turbochargers. Power output was 542bhp, and torque 475lb ft. In 1992, this was simply extraordinary, especially when all the power was transmitted to the rear wheels alone. The XJ220's performance, too, was stratospheric for the time: it took 3.8 seconds to reach 62mph and just 11.6 seconds to cross the 124mph barrier. Its claimed top speed was 213mph. Neither the 959 nor the F40 were, at the time, at the same level as the XJ220, and only the McLaren F1, with its 627bhp, managed to pulverize the Jaguar's performance two years later. What also helped this supercar achieve such levels of performance was its weight, which was just 1,470kg (3,241lb), thanks to a honeycomb aluminium structure that gave the body great structural rigidity.

The career of the XJ220 was to be quite short. Customers had to wait up to several years before taking delivery, because of the economic recession that put the brakes on orders in the early 1990s. Worldwide, the 275 units that were eventually produced remained on sale up until 1994.

XJ220

With 542bhp and a weight of 1,470kg (3,241lb), the XJ220 could reach 124mph in 11.6 seconds.

Jaguar XJ220, 1992

DISPLACEMENT: V6, 3,498cc; **MAX POWER :** 542bhp; **TORQUE:** 475lb ft; twin turbochargers; rear-wheel drive; five-speed manual gearbox; **WEIGHT:** 1,470kg (3,241lb).

XJS
1991

Reminiscence

Before 1991, the XJS was called the XJ-S... sometimes, with Jaguar, it's all about subtlety. After its launch in 1975, the XJ-S had a devil of a job erasing the memory of the E-type, which it had replaced. And reliability problems linked to its big V12 engine did nothing to help its reputation. At the start of the 1980s, sales of the XJ-S could be counted on the fingers of a few hands. However, John Egan, Jaguar's boss, still believed in it. He asked his team to improve the coupé's build quality, and called upon the engineer Michael May to give it an engine worthy of its standing. The new 5.3-litre V12, with "Fireball"-type cylinder head (featuring high-turbulence combustion chambers), was the result. It went on sale in 1981. Two years later, a new six-cylinder, 3.6-litre engine was developed and offered in the XJ-S. Sales gradually recovered.

But people only really started talking about the series in 1989, with the extravagant XJR-S, developed with Jaguar's endurance racing team, TWR. Thanks to an increased piston stroke length, the original big V12 was turned into a 6-litre version. The entire upper part of the engine – cylinder heads, cylinders and pistons – was redesigned.

In 1991, with the XJ-S making way for the XJS, came the final transformation, consisting of a radical facelift inside and out, including a new dashboard. A considerable leap was made in build quality. Two years later, the standard V12 was increased to 6 litres capacity (313bhp), and the inline six to 4 litres (238bhp). In the summer of 1996, after the limited "Celebration" edition, the last XJSs rolled off the production line, ending a run of some 115,500 over 20 years.

OPPOSITE
The XJR-S produced 333bhp. Its spoiler was a testament to its racing ambitions.

Jaguar XJS V12, 1991

DISPLACEMENT: V12, 5,343cc; **MAX POWER:** 280bhp; **TORQUE:** 306lb ft; naturally aspirated; rear-wheel drive; five-speed manual gearbox or automatic; **WEIGHT:** 1,755kg (3,869lb).

Chapter 5

HISTORY

An American accent

1987 › 2007

The privatization of Jaguar in 1984 – which saw it leave British Leyland and become Jaguar Car Holdings – and its recovery over five years under the leadership of Sir John Egan attracted the keen interest of large motor industry groups. Jaguar had stabilized its finances, essentially thanks to cost-cutting and redundancies (which involved around 10,000 employees) but also to a more aggressive business approach. Dealers had to pay for vehicles over very short periods, which resulted in increasing Jaguar's cash flow.

On the factory floor, relations between management and staff were still strained. Nevertheless, Egan had been anxious to keep production in Castle Bromwich and improve the factory's productivity. However, sales of the XJ40, which had been in production since 1986, did not achieve the hoped-for volume, despite several years of marketing. The model had suffered because of the unreliability of the early versions, in spite of the attention paid to build quality. Many employees lacked training. Within the company, people were sometimes wondering whether it would have been preferable to continue even longer with production of the XJ6 Series III, whose late versions had sold well. But Egan wanted to move forward. Later, though, he declared: "We understood, rather belatedly, that it was much harder than we thought to launch a new model as technologically

advanced as the XJ40. It wasn't because the car wasn't very robust. The problem lay in setting up a manufacturing process that matched the original intentions at the design stage. I suppose it's fair to say we were inexperienced."

At the end of the 1980s, Jaguar no longer had the resources to invest in research and development. The AJ6 six-cylinder engine, which had succeeded the XK, was now at the end of its life, German competition was vigorous, and the Japanese were entering the US market with new, prestigious brands such as the Lexus, which was owned by Toyota. Egan, whom the press had previously praised, no longer had the same aura about him. Nevertheless, it was decided to increase the displacement of the "old" AJ6 in 1989. It went up to 4 litres, achieving a power output of 223bhp, a considerable boost for the XJ40. But the economies of the richest countries were on a downturn and, at the very end of the 1980s, British companies were suffering from an unfavourable exchange rate for the pound against the dollar – during the 1970s, a Jaguar cost only some $10,000 more than a Cadillac, whereas ten years later this difference had risen to $20,000. Jaguar's share price was plunging, and the Thatcher government was looking favourably on potential buyers, which were starting to prowl around the company. "Over the years we were contacted by most of the world's big car manufacturers," John Egan said after leaving

Robert Knight, the legendary engineer, started at Jaguar in 1944. He launched the XJ40 project, then retired. He died in 2000.

Sir John Egan, squatting on the right, celebrating the release of the 100,000th XJ (an XJ40) with Jaguar plant workers in September 1989.

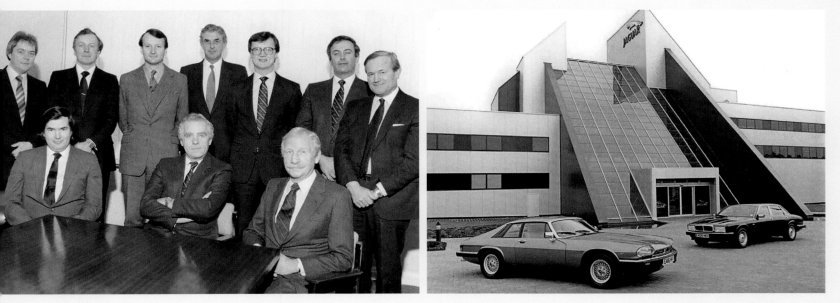

In the 1980s, John Egan (sitting centre-left) and his team were able to turn Jaguar into a profitable business, even though ten years before, the situation had seemed, in his own words, "hopeless".

Jaguar. "Each time we explained why we wanted to remain independent, and I must say that many people respected that."

However, at the end of 1989, intentions became clearer. General Motors, one of Jaguar's suppliers and a US giant, wanted to acquire a share of the British marque. Ford quickly made a counteroffer. The government suddenly removed the "golden share" (which prevented any shareholder acquiring more than 15 per cent of Jaguar) on 31 October 1989, after Ford had announced its desire to buy Jaguar outright. The latter's share price immediately rose. Ford concluded the acquisition in haste, without even visiting the factory! The deal was for £1.6bn, five times Jaguar's market value, and was sealed after a night of frantic negotiation between Egan and Morgan, Grenfell & Co. representing Jaguar, and Goldman Sachs representing Ford.

Why had the US company been in such a hurry to acquire Jaguar? Because it wanted at all costs to possess a luxury car brand, both for its home market and for the European one. It also believed it could improve Jaguar's profitability by modernizing its manufacturing tools, rationalizing its model range and optimizing quality control. Egan had never looked favourably on the arrival of Ford. He left the company in March 1990 to serve as the chief executive of the British Airports Authority. That same year, Margaret Thatcher left the government …

Egan's successor, William Hayden, came from Ford Europe. As soon as he arrived, he saw how dilapidated Jaguar's factories were, and had these words for the press: "The only factory I've visited that was in a more pitiful state was in Gorky, in Soviet Russia!" His abrasive style was not to everyone's taste, but he implemented radical reforms that would soon bear fruit. Happily, the vice-chair, John Grant, was more measured, but he could do nothing to stop Hayden's determination to push the engineer Jim Randle, who had created the XJ40, to the limits of his patience. Randle ended up leaving

Jaguar, to be replaced by Clive Ennos. The new boss then set about outsourcing design, which alienated design chief Geoff Lawson.

Bob Dover was appointed director of engineering, and a vast model renewal programme was launched. At the same time, 4,000 staff were made redundant or offered early retirement. However, if Ford had not taken over Jaguar, it is a safe bet that the marque would have vanished. The company was losing up to £1m per day in the early 1990s! Hayden remained at the head of the company for only two years, and was succeeded by Nick Scheele, who stayed in post until 1999.

In 1993, the XJ40 was given a V12 engine. The design of the XJS was improved, and a version fitted with the large 6-litre V12 engine appeared. Also, plans for a replacement for the XJ40 were finalized. These new plans differed from the project previously set up by Randle (for the XJ90 prototype), which had been more ambitious. From a style point of view, the X300 (this was its codename) was reminiscent of the Series III, which had been so well liked. At its launch in the autumn of 1994, the new XJ consigned the XJ40 to the history books. But its soul lived on, forming the basis not only of the X300 (the AJ16 engine was derived from the AJ6) but also of the V8-engined X308 model, which continued in production until 2002.

Over the years Jaguar renewed its range completely. The Ford era was a lifesaver, although there were significant sacrifices. In 2000, the arrival of the F-type was like a thunderclap, as were those of the S-type (1999) and X-type (2001). Ford had also set up, in 1999, the PAG (Premier Automotive Group) subsidiary to develop operations. Ford acquired Land Rover in 2000. A common dealer network was put in place. But in the mid-2000s the Ford Group began to go into decline. In 2006, it posted a record loss of $12.7bn (£10.01bn), of which $300m (£237m) was attributed to Jaguar Land Rover. Ford decided to sell both brands.

The Castle Bromwich plant, where most Jaguars were made from 1977 onward, was updated during the Ford years.

1990
Ford's main objective was to streamline Jaguar's production.

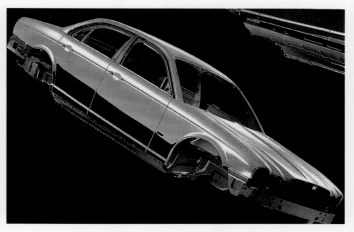

Bibiana Boerio became the head of Jaguar in 2004, after having cut her teeth at Ford. She released the new XK in 2005 at the Frankfurt Motor Show (shown here).

The XJ, produced in the mid-1990s, was a boon for Jaguar. It was the first model made under Ford's leadership.

The X-type, released in 2001, was a testament to the upheavals of the 2000s: it was the first diesel-powered Jaguar, and the first Jaguar to be made widely available as an estate car (station wagon).

X300

1994

A success!

Sales of the Jaguar XJ40 were hardly making management happy, the company's shareholders even less so, and the various reliability issues did not improve the car's image. Jaguar did not have the resources to invest in more modern manufacturing tools commensurate with the quality expected by the upmarket customers that were the company's target. When Ford expressed an interest in buying Jaguar in 1989, the British company's management were not thrilled, but the shareholders saw it as a godsend. The sale was completed in 1990. The new boss, William Hayden, quickly got production back in order.

In October 1994, the replacement for the XJ40 made its appearance, under the codename X300. It echoed the majestic lines of the original XJ6, which were successfully adapted to suit the standards of the 1990s. The two main elements prioritized during its design were reliability and a return to a traditional design typical of the marque – a task that the designer Geoff Lawson had been working on since 1991. In fact, the marketing department used the phrase "Back to the XJ Series". It was built using modern, robotized processes at the Browns Lane

factory. A total of £200m was invested in upgrading the manufacturing tools.

Three engines were offered: the AJ6 inline six-cylinder (3.2 litres, producing 219bhp, or 4 litres, producing 249bhp) for the X300; the 6-litre V12, producing 318bhp, for the X305; and the supercharged 4-litre, based on the six-cylinder AJ16, which produced 326bhp, for the X306. The last of these was fitted to the XJR, the sportiest XJ. British elegance was back with a fanfare.

The new XJ pitted itself against Audis, BMWs and Mercedes, but with that extra bit of British soul. The car's regal comfort – largely due to four-wheel independent suspension and the quality of the seats – prevailed over its sporting spirit. These models were rather heavy. The XJR itself was more reminiscent of a ship capable of high speed with a luxury interior than of a true sports car. The Daimler Double Six (known as Vanden Plas in the United States), even more cocooning and powered by the V12, had undergone the same modifications. In 1996, a convertible, named Daimler Corsica, was released. Finally, a Jaguar X330 was launched in 1995, offering what would subsequently become an

OPPOSITE

In addition to the base model and the Daimler Vanden Plas, the X300 was available in Executive, Sovereign, and Sport versions.

ABOVE
While the X300 engine was based on the XJ40, it benefitted from thoughtfully conceived improvements, especially with fuel injection.

RIGHT
Despite the streamlining of production, the very first X300s were missing a glove compartment due to a problem with the subcontractor.

option for all models (except the XJR): its wheelbase was extended by 15in (38cm). Most cars sold had a ZF four-speed automatic gearbox, even though manual versions were available.

The X300 proved to be more reliable than the XJ40, despite some teething troubles with the 1995 models, such as slight leaks at the cylinder head joint – which were fixed by replacements under warranty. The same went for oil pressure sensors and a few other faults. But the X300's big weak spot, over time, was the headliner, which sagged over the years, almost without exception.

Once again, credit is due to the designer Lawson, replaced in 1999 by Ian Callum. He succeeded in redesigning an XJ6 that powerfully evoked the first car that bore the name, with rounded lines and an air of timeless modernity – unlike the XJ40.

From the first year it was on sale, the X300 enabled Jaguar to increase its sales by 10 per cent worldwide. The arrival of Ford, therefore, seemed to yield fruits that may not have been exotic but were juicy none the less.

X300

This new XJ6 was a milestone in the history of the legendary saloon.

Jaguar X300, 1994

DISPLACEMENT: inline six-cylinder, 3,239cc; **MAX POWER:** 219bhp; **TORQUE:** 232lb ft; naturally aspirated; rear-wheel drive; five-speed manual gearbox or automatic; **WEIGHT :** 1,800kg (3,968lb).

XJR
1995

A true sports car?

The XJR was unveiled in 1995 as the high-performance model of the new XJ series, whose codename was X300. It was Jaguar's first vehicle with a supercharger, the chief advantage of which was that it increased torque rather than power. This seemed wise for a heavy, comfortable saloon. The power of the six-cylinder AJ16 engine was thus boosted to 326bhp, with 278lb ft of torque, thanks to the Eaton M90 supercharger, together with an intercooler. The XJR was fitted with 17in (43.2cm) wheels, whereas the rest of the range featured 16in (40.6cm) wheels. The XJR also featured sportier suspension, to improve roadholding when driving fast. It was also available with a five-speed Getrag manual gearbox, although the vast majority of XJRs sold had the GM 4L80-E automatic. Despite these features and several aesthetic tweaks (for example, a body-coloured radiator grille, bigger tailpipes, special "Sport" five-spoke alloy wheels and an XJR badge), the XJR was never really considered a truly sporty car by the public. And yet, it shared the base of its engine with the DB7 from Aston Martin – a marque also owned by Ford at the time. The engine was tuned by TWR.

Be that as it may, Jeremy Clarkson, presenter of *Top Gear*, was unstinting in his praise after a test drive of the XJR in 1995: "I realized 'good' was too small a word. Senbleedingsational is better... This car is astonishing."

OPPOSITE
The XJR was the first mass-produced Jaguar with a supercharger.

Jaguar XJR, 1995

DISPLACEMENT: inline six-cylinder, 3,980cc; **MAX POWER:** 326bhp; **TORQUE:** 378lb ft; supercharged; rear-wheel drive; five-speed manual gearbox or automatic; **WEIGHT:** 1,800kg (3,968lb).

XK8

1996

Rejuvenation

Jaguar absolutely had to reinvent itself. It was the second half of the 1990s, and Porsche was on the point of scoring a massive hit with the 911 Type 996, which shared almost half its components with the Boxster – a car that was selling like hot cakes. Jaguar then unveiled the XK8. This coupé, with its rounded lines, referenced the E-type much more than the XJS coupé, which by this time was looking a little dated.

It was 1996, and coupés were proliferating on the market, from both luxury and mass-market manufacturers. The XK8 made its mark as one of the most voluptuous-looking coupés you could buy. While the competition tended to favour an angular look, Jaguar opted for a particularly elegant design. This 2+2 GT gave the brand an injection of youthfulness, but some of the controls, which were from Ford, came in for criticism. Elements such as the climate control and GPS controls, as well as the shape of the key, were cases in point. Nevertheless, this was undoubtedly a true Jaguar, from the very vertical dashboard, with its premium wood veneer, and the seats, which offered a high level of comfort.

Since Ford was the parent company, build quality had to be impeccable. All the little niggles, including the electrics, for which British cars were well known in earlier decades, became a distant memory with the XK8. People also overlooked the limited space devoted to the rear seats, for the ambience on board was worthy of the finest British cars of the day. In this respect, it could be argued that even Aston Martin was lagging behind a bit.

At its launch in 1996, Jaguar fitted the XK8 with a 4-litre V8 engine that produced 294bhp. Hot on its heels came the XK8 Convertible and the XKR. The latter used the same V8 engine but it was supercharged to produce 375bhp. The XKR coupé was easily recognizable, thanks to its more pointed front end, featuring a special radiator grille and lateral bonnet vents.

While the XK8 was a lovely car just for going for a drive, the XKR had a much more sporty and brutal temperament as regards its handling. It was nevertheless very comfortable for a sports car, boasting almost 400bhp. The coupé brought to mind a big, very elegant grand tourer, whereas the convertible had a rather more classic look on the road. At a time when coupé–convertibles

OPPOSITE
The XK8 Jaguar remains one of the most elegant coupés available, even after 20 years.

ABOVE
The XKR convertible made it possible to fully appreciate the rather husky sound of the supercharged V8.

RIGHT
The XK was among the last Jaguar coupés made with large areas of high-quality wood veneer.

were proliferating, the XK8 convertible made do with a canvas soft top, which avoided the visual ungainliness of a retractable hard-top mechanism at the rear.

In 2002, the XK was restyled, with a number of very small touches. It was quite difficult to modify such flowing lines, so it was on the technical side that the XK was modified the most. The naturally aspirated 4-litre V8 engine was boosted to 4.2 litres, giving the XK 304bhp and a 0–62mph time of 6.6 seconds. The XKR's supercharged V8 went from 375 to 406bhp, with acceleration 0–62mph in just 5.6 seconds. But the most distinctive thing about this version of the XKR was the exceptional sound of its supercharged V8, which resembled more the sounds on a US highway than an English country lane. Computer Active Technology Suspension (CATS) was fitted as standard, giving the car excellent handling. From 1996 to 2005, more than 90,000 XK8 variants were sold worldwide.

XK8

The first generation of XKs made many on-screen appearances, notably in the *Austin Powers* trilogy.

Jaguar XK8, 1996 **DISPLACEMENT:** V8, 3,996cc; **MAX POWER:** 294bhp; **TORQUE:** 290lb ft; naturally aspirated; rear-wheel drive; five-speed automatic gearbox; **WEIGHT:** 1,615kg (3,560lb).

X308

1997

The best?

Perhaps one of the most noteworthy events at Jaguar during the 1990s and 2000s was the launch of its V8 engine (known as project AJ26). The Audis, Mercedes and, above all, Lexus cars that featured this kind of engine were a thorn in the side of engineers at Jaguar and Ford. The original aim of the project had been to use an engine common to both marques, designed by Ford. But engineer Clive Ennos was opposed to this idea, and managed to convince management that a Jaguar car was duty-bound to have an engine worthy of its superior status. His team, therefore, started with a blank sheet of paper. Various options were contemplated – including an extraordinary two-stroke V6 producing 320bhp! The V8 engine eventually prevailed as a more rational solution.

The first V8, with a displacement of 4 litres, made its debut in the Jaguar XK8 and the new XJ, named the X308. The latter differed little from the X300, whose chassis it shared. Its design had been modernized, with a new, more delicate radiator grille. Despite everything, it retained the famous look of the first XJ6. Unveiled in 1997, the X308 stood out because of its V8 engines, which were offered with a range of displacements, from 3.2 to 5 litres. The sportiest version, the XJR, was given a 4-litre engine fitted with an Eaton supercharger; it boasted 375bhp. It remains a marvellous car: comfortable, powerful and reliable. As well as the standard XJ models, other levels of trim were available in the Sovereign, Executive and SE. In 2001, an XJR 100 was produced in a limited edition of just 500, for the centenary of Sir William Lyons' birth.

OPPOSITE
The X308 was cut from the same cloth as the first XJ6 and updated to suit modern needs.

Jaguar X308, 1997

DISPLACEMENT: V8, 3,248cc; **MAX POWER:** 240bhp; **TORQUE:** 233lb ft; naturally aspirated; rear-wheel drive; five-speed manual gearbox or automatic; **WEIGHT:** 1,754kg (3,867lb).

XK180
1998

An unfinished dream?

At the 1998 Paris Motor Show, people crowded round the Jaguar stand to catch a glimpse of a superb concept car called the XK180. Developed by Browns Lane's Special Vehicle Operations (SVO) workshop, the XK180 marked the 50th anniversary of the XK120. Based on the XKR, this concept car was a roadster with a very shallow windscreen and a double bulge at the rear that referenced the very beautiful D-type of the 1950s. It was Keith Helfet, designer of another automotive work of art, the XJ220, who was given the honour of designing this concept car.

Under the XK180's bonnet was the supercharged 4-litre V8 that powered the production XKR, but its output was boosted to 450bhp. It was connected to an automatic gearbox, but with steering wheel-mounted push buttons for sequential gear changes. The XK180 was lighter than the XKR, thanks to its all-aluminium body made by Abbey Panels. This US-based supplier had also worked on the bodywork for the C-type, D-type, XJ13 and XJ220. Brembo provided the braking system, which featured aluminium four-piston calipers and cross-drilled, ventilated rotors at the front. These large discs sat behind enormous 20in wheels – the biggest ever fitted to a Jaguar at that time.

Contrary to what you might think, the XK180 was only ever a concept car, and Jaguar never brought it into production. Although it is possible, very rarely, to encounter one on the road, these are simply replicas that are faithful to the original to a greater or lesser extent. Jaguar built only two prototypes, for international car shows.

OPPOSITE
The XK 180 was without a doubt one of the most successful concept cars Jaguar ever released. While many copies exist, only two XK180s were ever made.

S-Type
1998

The "baby Jaguar"

OPPOSITE

While its name made reference to the 1963 models, the shape of the S-type Jaguar paid tribute to the Mark 2 saloons of the 1960s.

In 1996, when the XK8 coupé went on sale, Jaguar needed to offer a saloon that was less top-of-the-range than the XJ. Since the launch of the large XJ saloon in 1968, the company had not brought out a smaller saloon. Jaguar then needed a mass-market saloon, especially in a world market where saloon touring cars accounted for the majority of high-end car manufacturers' sales. The challenge was to compete with models such as BMW's 5 Series, the Mercedes E-Class and the Audi A6.

The S-type was unveiled at the British International Motor Show in Birmingham in 1998. Although its name paid tribute to the 1963 S-type, its lines were much more reminiscent of the Mark 2 saloon. This touring car had a very rounded profile, with large areas of glass, a sloping roofline and a tapered rear. It was an excellent marriage between the essence of the legendary 1960s saloon and the modernity the company was seeking on the eve of the 21st century. The car had an elegant, rather refined profile that drew the eye. Its front end featured round headlights, which were very fashionable at the time, but the radiator grille differed from the rest of the Jaguar range – unlike those of the XK8 coupé and the XJ, it was oval.

Once on board, anyone familiar with fine British cars would have felt quickly at home, thanks to the vertical dashboard, fine wood veneers that were very much in evidence and, of course, the high-quality leather upholstery. But there were also features that came from Ford, such as the central console containing the audio system, the GPS and the climate control buttons. Nevertheless, Jaguar had found a way to integrate everything effectively.

Even though at the time it was, rather too glibly, dubbed the "baby Jaguar", the S-type soon proved itself to be a true "living room on wheels". It was known for its generous interior and level of equipment, as well as its perfect build quality. At the time, German competitors already offered very long lists of costly options, whereas Jaguar wanted to compete aggressively on price – to the point that the S-type rivalled touring cars from mass-market manufacturers, notably the Renault Safrane and Peugeot 605 which, in 1999, were ageing.

The S-type was also available with a good range of engines. In came a new 3-litre, 243bhp,

S-Type
Although known as the "baby Jaguar," the S-type was by no means a base model.

OPPOSITE, TOP
Apart from the chrome grille, there was no indication that this S-type R could produce 406hp.

OPPOSITE, BOTTOM
The interior of the S-type was generous, both in terms of space and amenities.

ABOVE
Although the S-type was criticized for using Ford parts, such as the navigation system, riding it felt like being in a real Jaguar.

ABOVE
When it launched, the S-type was undeniably one of the most elegant saloons available.

OPPOSITE
Although technically not a sports car, the S-type R ran much like a real GT.

petrol V6. It was followed by the 4.2-litre V8 from the XK8, which produced 285bhp. Being 100kg (220lb) heavier than the V6 S-type, this V8 version did not offer significantly more performance. Subsequently, the range of engines was expanded with the S-type R, whose supercharged 4.2-litre V8 produced 406bhp and was combined with a six-speed automatic gearbox.

As seen with the various brands in the Volkswagen group, the S-type fitted in completely with Ford's policy of platform sharing. The car borrowed its platform from an American model, the Lincoln LS. Jaguar purists, however, were soon reassured by the new car's excellent chassis and on-road comfort. Even though it was not really meant to make its mark as a radical sports saloon, the S-type, even in its R version, offered handling worthy of a grand tourer. Faced with competitors that were often aesthetically more radical, the S-type enabled its owner to drive a British car that was more discreet, but with a strong personality.

S-Type

When the S-type was first launched, it had a much lower price tag than those of its German rivals.

Jaguar S-Type 4.0 V8, 1998 — **DISPLACEMENT:** V8, 3,996cc; **MAX POWER:** 295bhp; **TORQUE:** 288lb ft; naturally aspirated; rear-wheel drive; five-speed automatic gearbox; **WEIGHT:** 1,725 kg (3,803lb).

Jaguar competed in the 85 Grand Prix, podiumed twice, and came seventh in three consecutive seasons.

A career cut short

| 2000-2004 |

During the 1990s, the Ford Motor Company put in place a strategy that allocated its marques to different areas of motorsport. Aston Martin took part in the World Endurance Championship, and the acquisition of Cosworth, in 1998, allowed Ford to become more deeply involved in Formula One through the Stewart Grand Prix team. Ford acquired the team outright in 1999, renaming it Jaguar Racing. It entered the Formula One World Championship in the 2000 season.

Jaguar Racing went on to produce five generations of single-seater cars (from the Jaguar R1 to the R5) and quickly produced results, finishing seventh in the Constructors' Championship for three consecutive seasons. Numerous changes within the team's management, followed by a cut in the budget, led the constructor to leave Formula One at the end of the 2004 season. In 2005, Jaguar Racing was bought Red Bull Racing. In 2016, Jaguar returned to single-seater racing, but this time in Formula E.

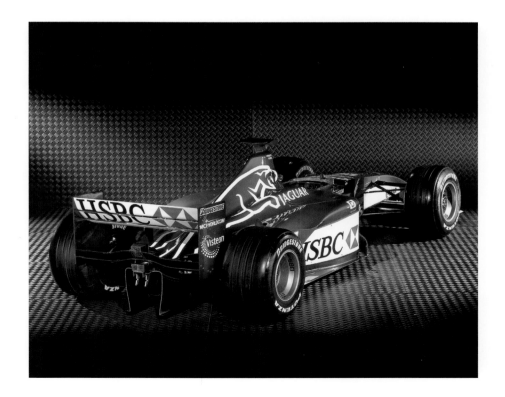

ABOVE
In 2004, Mark Webber scored seven points at the wheel of a Jaguar R5. The Jaguar Racing team finished seventh for the third season in a row, with a total of ten points.

X-Type
2001

Unloved

The year was 2001. Despite the existence of the XJ large saloon, the XK coupé and convertible, as well as the S-type saloon touring car, Jaguar wanted to complete its range with an even more affordable saloon. In order to do this, the company rummaged in the Ford parts bin and pulled out the platform of the very latest Mondeo Estate. The X-type was born.

This saloon competed with the BMW 3 Series, Mercedes C-Class and Audi A4. Despite its close family ties with the second-generation Ford Mondeo (at the time one of the best family saloons from mass-market manufacturers) the X-type had, from the outside, nothing of the Ford about it. With its four headlamps, whose rounded shape protruded forward, following the line of the fluted bonnet, the X-type was a stylish, elegant saloon – a true Jaguar. Inside, the X-type came in for criticism over the controls, which did resemble those in the Mondeo.

This was unfair because, if those critics had bothered to take a look at Ferrari at that time, they would have come across a few surprises from Fiat. Regardless, the X-type was not short of equipment.

Aside from its codename, X400, the "X" in X-type referenced a major revolution in Jaguar's history: four-wheel drive. At its launch, the X-type was available only in this guise, and with two V6 petrol engines: a 2.5-litre producing 197bhp and a 3-litre producing 234hp. Although it was very stable in the wet, the X-type's handling was nevertheless more understeering than rear-wheel drive (it tended to behave more like a front-wheel drive) – another detail that did not go down well with Jaguar purists.

Jaguar had been counting on producing 100,000 X-types per year but the company never exceeded 60,000 at best, even though it introduced diesel engines to the range, as well as an estate car – another first for the manufacturer.

OPPOSITE
Despite its natural elegance, the X-type was a commercial failure.

Jaguar X-Type 3.0 V6, 2001

DISPLACEMENT: V6, 2,967cc; **MAX POWER:** 234bhp; **TORQUE:** 209lb ft; naturally aspirated; four-wheel drive; five-speed manual gearbox or automatic gearbox; **WEIGHT:** 1,660kg (3,660lb).

XJ (X350)

2003

The modernized XJ

In 2003, Jaguar completely updated the XJ. It must be said that the flagship of the range was badly in need of it – not so much in its design, which was simply timeless, but rather technically. BMW had just launched a completely new 7 Series, featuring the first SOS button, as well as an onboard entertainment system controlled by an unusual dial (i-Drive), and Audi had totally revised its all-aluminium A8. It was precisely this light material that was used by Jaguar to build its new flagship car.

The construction process was more costly because it required, among other things, more than 3,000 rivets to assemble a single XJ. It also employed an epoxy gluing technique pioneered by Lotus on its Elise model a few years earlier. When all was said and done, the structure of this 5.09m (16¾ft)-long saloon was 60 per cent more rigid and 40 per cent lighter than that of the previous XJ. This meant that the new XJ had an unladen weight of slightly more than 1,600kg (3,500lb), or 200kg (441lb) less than the previous generation XJ, whereas its rivals, such as the Mercedes S-Class and BMW 7 Series, could easily top 2 tonnes. The

new generation XJ even managed to be a little lighter than the new aluminium Audi A8.

Jaguar did not aim to revolutionize the lines of its new XJ, especially as customers who bought this type of vehicle did not tend to appreciate major stylistic changes. It made sense that the shape, which dated from 1968, should be retained, even after 35 years. The front of the car was very similar to the previous XJ, although more imposing, with four round headlights. The car's outline, however, was slightly different. While the previous XJ appeared to crouch low on the ground, the new car was 9cm (3½in) taller. Its extra bulk was obvious, with both its width and length increased by 6cm (2¼in).

The main advantage of the aluminium construction was a weight saving, which had several benefits. The fact that this big saloon was lighter allowed it to be nimbler on the road, use less fuel and also be more comfortable, thanks to the adoption of suspension settings that had less weight to support – that is, were less firm. Despite a length of 5.09m (16¾ft), this XJ offered slightly sportier handling than previous generations.

OPPOSITE
The XJ (X350) borrowed the spirit of previous XJ models, but it was longer, wider and taller.

XJ (X350)

It was the first XJ to be equipped with a 100 per cent aluminium body.

OPPOSITE, TOP
The XJ never failed to use high-quality parts. The company's skill was always very much on display.

OPPOSITE, BOTTOM
The XJ was longer than its predecessor, and offered more space for its occupants.

ABOVE
The XJR was easily recognizable due to its unique grille and its wide-diameter wheels.

ABOVE
Thanks to its structure and its aluminium body, the XJ was lighter than many of its rivals.

OPPOSITE
The XJ V8 remains a paragon of reliability.

182

Naturally, comfort was still important, and the car had pneumatic suspension (CATS), which constantly monitored the shock absorbers' settings according to the driving style adopted.

Underneath the bonnet, the entry-level engine was a V6 producing 243bhp, but the XJ also came with 3.5- and 4.2-litre V8 engines, producing 265bhp and 304bhp respectively. Finally, a 4.2-litre,

V8 producing 406bhp, the XJR, topped the range. This sportier version was not necessarily a car that you would race on the track, but it must be admitted that the XJR remains one of the most impressive large saloons today and one of the most enjoyable to drive. It should also be noted that the 4.2-litre V8 was remarkably reliable – as long as it was properly looked after, just like any other engine.

XJ (X350)

This generation of XJs was the last to be built in the shape designed in 1968.

Jaguar XJ (X350) 4.2 V8, 2003 **DISPLACEMENT:** V8, 4,196cc; **MAX POWER:** 304bhp; **TORQUE:** 310lb ft; naturally aspirated; rear-wheel drive; six-speed automatic gearbox; **WEIGHT:** 1,609kg (3,547lb).

XK
2006

More radical

In 2006, Jaguar launched a completely new generation of the XK coupé. The XK8 had been in production for almost ten years and, even if it still appealed from the outside, its interior was becoming very dated.

The new coupé, called XK, was designed by Ian Callum, creator of the Aston Martin DB7 and Vanquish. Although on the outside reminiscent of its predecessor, rather like the Aston coupés from Newport Pagnell, the new XK coupé stood out with its imposing stature and taut, sporty lines. Its long, fluted bonnet, which ended with a wider radiator grille, was also impressive.

The inside was also extensively modernized. Of course, in general terms, the essence of the marque remained, with the elegant, vertical dashboard, but there was a minor revolution. For the first time, it was possible not to have wood veneer in a Jaguar!

Customers could opt for aluminium – or rather, aluminium-style – panelling. As well as applying to the numerous chromed elements, this applied to the gear selector and the control levers, too. But, above all, there was leather everywhere in this handsome cabin, designed for two or, occasionally, four people – for the two rear seats were still seats in name only.

Under the bonnet, the new XK initially featured the 4.2-litre V8, producing 298bhp. This was soon replaced by a 5-litre V8, which boosted output to 385bhp. The R version initially attained 426bhp with the 4.2-litre V8; this increased to 510bhp with the supercharged 5-litre engine. What impressed immediately was the car's extremely raucous sound, which brought to mind American V8 engines. This was no coincidence, for Jaguar wanted to appeal to precisely that market.

OPPOSITE
The second generation of XKR coupés boasted a far sportier look than that of its predecessors.

Jaguar XK, 2008

DISPLACEMENT: V8, 5,000cc; **MAX POWER:** 510bhp; **TORQUE:** 461lb ft; supercharged; rear-wheel drive; six-speed automatic gearbox; **WEIGHT:** 1,753kg (3,865lb).

Chapter 6

HISTORY

The Indian era

2008 › 2019

On 1 January 2008, Ford, which wanted to part company with Jaguar Land Rover (JLR), officially declared that the Indian group Tata was the most suitable candidate to take over the British marques. Tata also secured the agreement of the British trades union TGWU-Amicus (now Unite), the main union representing workers in the British car industry. However, this announcement did not disqualify other potential candidates. On 18 March, Reuters news agency revealed that the American banks Citigroup and J P Morgan would finance any potential transaction with a $2.5bn (£1.97bn) loan.

On 26 March 2008, Ford announced that it had agreed to sell its interest in Jaguar and Land Rover to Tata Motors of India, which planned to finalize the sale by the end of the second quarter of 2008. The agreement included the rights to three other British brands linked to Jaguar: Daimler, Lanchester and Rover. On 2 June 2008, the sale of JLR to Tata was concluded for the sum of £1.7bn ($2.16bn).

Colossus

The British brand's future would from now on be played out in India, a former British colony and a member of the Commonwealth. Nevertheless, Tata formed a subsidiary, Jaguar Land Rover Automotive PLC, whose headquarters were in Whitley, near Coventry. The huge Indian group was founded in 1868. In 2008, it was run by Ratan Naval Tata, a descendant of the founder. The bulk of the company's operations were in steel, IT, telecommunications, tea (through the Tetley brand) and hotels (through the Taj brand). But it quickly became involved in transport, with utility and commercial vehicles, and, subsequently, touring cars (through the TELCO Group) – in 1954 Tata had formed a joint venture with Daimler Benz to produce commercial cars. In 1991, buoyed by its years dominating the Indian market, Tata Motors launched its first touring car: the Tata Sierra. It was followed by the Tata Estate in 1992, the Tata Sumo two years later and the Tata Safari in 1998. However, success came only with the Tata Indica, also launched in 1998 and exported to several countries, including South Africa. The company then planned to break into the luxury car market – but in order to do so, it needed a name.

This was a done deal by 2008, when Tata got its hands on Jaguar and Land Rover. Of course, the acquisition involved some upheavals within management. Geoff Polites, the head of JLR since 2005, would certainly have been involved, but sadly cancer claimed his life at the age of 61, before Tata had found a successor. This needed to be done urgently. David Smith, who was with the company during the Ford era, was put in charge of JLR, although he remained in post for only two years. Carl Peter Forster, who came from General Motors, was appointed as the new head of Tata Motors. These changes demonstrated Tata's desire to become a force in the car manufacturing sector.

Ratan Naval Tata remained at the helm of Tata until 2012. He negotiated with Ford to acquire Jaguar.

In March 2012, Jaguar Land Rover and Chery, a Chinese automaker, sealed a deal to collaborate on the production of Jaguar and Land Rover cars and engines in China. The deal resulted in the opening of the Changshu plant.

The Pune plant, in India, opened in 2011, three years after Tata acquired Jaguar. The research and development centre remained in Coventry.

The car world was now eager to know what direction Jaguar would take. It did not have long to wait before a new model caused a stir. A new XJ, codenamed X351, was unveiled in July 2009. Its design was a radical break from the conservative approach seen until then. It departed from the lines of the first XJ of 1968, veering more toward the XF, which had itself come from the C-XF prototype. Its entirely digital dashboard, contained in an enormous panoramic screen (Jaguar iTech), bore witness to the quest for modernity by the team of stylists, still led by Ian Callum, the marque's star designer. The lines of the big, aluminium-bodied saloon displayed fewer curves and aimed to look more aggressive, ready to take on BMWs and Audis. Several engines were available, including a 3-litre diesel V6 and a 5-litre petrol V8. It was not to everyone's taste – especially not to the more conservative – but this new XJ gave the marque new momentum and opened up numerous possibilities. There was nowhere Jaguar could not go.

Less than a year after the appearance of the XJ X351, David Smith left his post at the head of Jaguar for personal reasons. It was a German, Ralf Dieter Speth, who took the reins. He had cut his teeth at BMW before being taken on by Jaguar in the PAG Group set up by Ford. In 2013, another German, Wolfgang Ziebart, joined Jaguar as head of the engineering division. None of this was coincidental – Germans were renowned for their qualities as managers and engine designers. Their country's motor industry was the jewel of the world's car manufacturing. Now, Tata hoped to encroach on their turf with Jaguar, especially in large markets such as China and the United States.

New models

The XJ had already been updated, in 2012, and several prototypes had mapped out the future, including the C-X75, which was unveiled at the Paris Motor Show in 2010, and the C-X16, revealed

at the Frankfurt motor show in 2011, with its sporty hybrid engine and lines that foreshadowed the future F-type. The XE replaced the X-type, revealing the ambitions of the Tata Group. At the end of 2014, Callum was awarded the Minerva Medal, given to the most creative designers, for automotive design. But the shock came in 2015 (the Jaguar marque's 80th anniversary) with the unveiling of the C-X17 concept car, which would lead to the F-Pace crossover. With this modern car, which had the looks of a classy SUV, Jaguar was demonstrating a crossover with its cousin Land Rover (and especially Range Rover). In 2015, Andy Goss, Jaguar Land Rover Global Sales Director, called the F-Pace "the ultimate practical sports car – a car that builds on the marque's founding ideals of grace, pace and space to become one of the most innovative Jaguars we've ever developed."

Jaguar's strategy seemed effective: looking to the future but without denying the past (in 2014, the company had bought 153 classic cars from the world's largest private collection, including a Mark X that had belonged to Sir William Lyons). In 2017, the Jaguar Land Rover Group broke its own sales record, with 621,109 vehicles sold (a 7 per cent increase), including 178,601 Jaguar cars (an increase of 20 per cent). However, 2018 proved to be less rosy, essentially because of a slowdown in the Chinese market (which was down 21.6 per cent), but also as a result of new regulations applying to diesel vehicles and the possible consequences of Brexit. In early 2019, Speth announced cost-cutting measures, founded on a plan for 4,500 redundancies in England. "We are taking decisive action to help deliver long-term growth, in the face of multiple geopolitical and regulatory disruptions as well as technology challenges facing the automotive industry," he declared in a statement. Jaguar was again entering a difficult period. Not for the first time – or the last.

Ralf Dieter Speth joined Ford in 2007 as director of production and quality control. He was made CEO of Jaguar in November 2010.

2010 ❯ 2015
Between 2010 and 2015, Jaguar hired 17,000 employees.

The Jaguar I-Pace was voted Car of the Year in 2019. The brand's legendary designer, Ian Callum, accepted the award at the Geneva Motor Show, where the E-type had been unveiled in 1961.

In 2018, a research and development centre opened in Shannon, Ireland. It focused on "green" engines.

As a way to celebrate the XJ's 60th anniversary in 2018, Jaguar rounded up a large number of XJ cars from all years.

XF
2008

New features, for every model

OPPOSITE

The XF was responsible for Jaguar's true revival in 2008. Many of its features were reproduced in later models.

The year 2008 saw a number of changes at Jaguar. While sales had been falling for some time, and Ford had to sell the company following an unprecedented recession in the United States, Jaguar launched the XF. A replacement for the S-type, the XF was the first saloon launched under Jaguar's new owner, Tata Motors. At BMW and Mercedes, the 5 Series and E-Class respectively were technological leaders, and Jaguar re-entered the fray by hitting back with an innovative, seductive saloon.

Visually, the XF was the company's first saloon with the profile of a four-door coupé, and it came just a few years after Mercedes had inaugurated the trend with the CLS, making the Jaguar XF the second high-end saloon/coupé in the history of the motorcar. Designed under the direction of Ian Callum (who also created the first Aston Martin Vanquish and the range that followed it in the early 2000s), the XF was a visual triumph, somewhat resembling an XK coupé that had been stretched out into a saloon car.

No less remarkable was the interior, which introduced a number of elements that were later adopted across the whole Jaguar Land Rover range. This included the automatic transmission control, which took the form of a retractable gear selector set into the central console. Lightly touching the glove compartment caused it to open electrically; the same went for the ceiling lights. And, for the first time in a production car, music lovers could enjoy a Bowers & Wilkins sound system. All these small but completely unprecedented innovations would contribute to the XF's success.

Under the bonnet was a 4.2-litre V8 engine, available with two levels of power output: 298bhp or, in the XFR, 416bhp. From 2009, the 4.2-litre V8's displacement was increased to 5 litres; the supercharged version, on the XFR, produced 510bhp. A modified version of the XFR smashed

ABOVE
The Jaguar XF was characterized by a coupé-like shape. This touring car was among the first four-door saloon/coupés.

RIGHT
The 5-litre V8, which already graced XKR coupés and convertibles, allowed the XFR to produce 510bhp.

the Jaguar speed record – until then 217mph, held by the XJ220 – reaching 226mph. For its suspension, the XF borrowed many elements from the XK, and became one of the most effective saloons of its generation.

The car made its mark as soon as it was launched, with sales exceeding expectations. In its first full year, the XF sold twice as many units as the S-type. In 2012, the XF Sportbrake, an estate, was also launched, to offer customers more luggage space, which ranged from 550 to 1,675 litres (19½–59cu ft).

In 2015, the second generation XF boasted more elegant and, at the same time, more aggressive lines. The car's body was now 75 per cent aluminium. Derived from the XE saloon, this new platform made the XF the lightest saloon car in its category. Weighing almost 200kg (441lb) less than the first generation, this new XF was now more nimble and more comfortable on the road and, above all, had lower fuel consumption and CO_2 emissions. Also, some of its engines had been "downsized", with the 4.2-litre V8 dropped to make way for a new 3-litre V6, which was either naturally aspirated or supercharged. On top of all this, there was a multitude of electronic driving aids that rendered the car safer than ever. Although this saloon was at its best in its petrol version, it was the diesel, with a 2-litre four-cylinder engine (producing 163 or 180bhp), that met with the most success in Europe.

XF

Since the very beginning, the XF sold twice as many cars as the S-type it had replaced.

Jaguar XF, 2008

DISPLACEMENT: V8, 5,000cc; **MAX POWER:** 510bhp; **TORQUE:** 461lb ft; supercharged; rear-wheel drive; six-speed automatic gearbox; **WEIGHT:** 1,842kg (4,061lb).

XJ
2010

A revolution

In 2010, with Tata Motors now its parent company, the launch of a completely new XJ was a major turning point for Jaguar. The first executive saloon to be produced in the Tata Motors era, the XJ (type X351) was as if Porsche had decided to radically change its 911. This new XJ brought to an end – aesthetically speaking – a line of saloons and executive saloons that had started in 1968. More imposing and especially more futuristic than ever, this completely new line nevertheless retained the radiator grille typical of the marque. But the rest of the car's design was in no way reminiscent of the well-known XJ models that had preceded it.

Its overall shape was very different, and its profile was more akin to a hatchback than a three-box. The unstated aim was to gain a bigger market share in China, which was going crazy for large saloons. However, in Europe the new XJ was a little too revolutionary for Jaguar aficionados, and this model line, which brought to mind a very large coupé, did not really draw the crowds. Nevertheless, it comprised everything there was to like about an executive saloon of this level. With prestige wood veneers and luxurious leather, there was nothing to suggest that Jaguar had lost its soul. Moreover,

in comparison with BMW's 7 Series and Audi's A8, the XJ had largely caught up in terms of technology. Although the dashboard featured conventional-looking instruments, it was in fact completely digital, while the middle, upper part of the central console was dominated by a wide, colour touch-screen.

When travelling in this new XJ, the miles were devoured either in total silence, thanks to a level of soundproofing that was unprecedented from this manufacturer, or while enjoying the 1,200 watt Bowers & Wilkins sound system. In the back, the car still took perfect care of its guests, with seats that offered a high level of comfort. Of course, there were plenty of different options available, but even the base model was very generous in this regard.

Under the bonnet, there was an impressive engine line-up. As well as the diesel V6, which was popular in Europe, this XJ was available with petrol units such as the supercharged 3-litre V6 producing 345bhp and the supercharged 5-litre V8, pumping out 510bhp. Very quickly, Jaguar offered four-wheel drive for its executive saloon – a first for this car, which now allowed the driver to take on the bitterest weather with total peace of mind. Jaguar equipped its big saloon with a system that distributed power

OPPOSITE
The XJ (X351) put an end to more than 40 years of Jaguar's highly recognizable grille and profile. It was a defining moment for this great British cat.

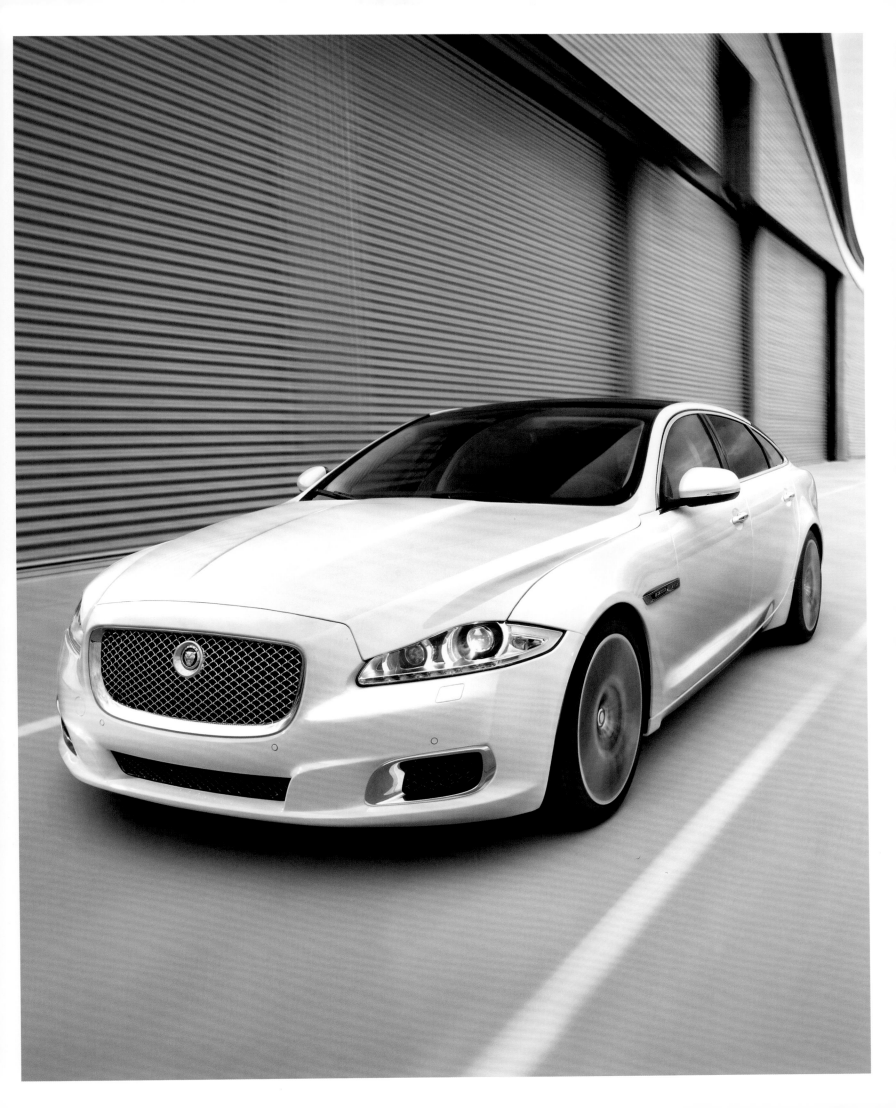

XJ

The 2010 XJ put an end to the aesthetics that had dominated since 1968.

OPPOSITE, TOP
While the XJ came with many sporty touches, notably with the R model. Its designers used a good number of chrome parts across the series.

OPPOSITE, BOTTOM
The back seat of this seventh generation XJ catered to its occupants down to the last detail. It was a true lounge/office on wheels.

ABOVE
The XJ (X351) dashboard had many standout features, including an LCD display.

ABOVE
A largely aluminium structure and body, and a very efficient all-wheel drive, allowed this lavish British limousine to provide its drivers with great agility, even in the snow.

RIGHT
The back seat of the XJ came with heated and ventilated seats, as well as a minibar.

up to 50/50 between the front and rear wheels. This meant that, while driving on snow, "kick-down" was now possible without the risk of fishtailing – but, reassuringly, this XJ nevertheless retained its rear-wheel-drive character. Unlike the X-type from ten years previously, the new module for transferring torque (Transfer Case Control Module – TCCM) prioritized the rear wheels by default, which rendered the car more pleasant to drive in all conditions. Even the non-AWD version of this XJ turned out to be highly effective on country lanes, thanks to its air suspension at the rear and a front end that steered very precisely. Jaguar had managed to produce an executive saloon 5.13m (16¾ft) long and weighing close to 1.8 tonnes that was almost as nimble as a compact saloon on twisting roads.

In 2015, the XJ was given a facelift, acquiring LED headlamps that, when lit, made a "J" shape. Inside, technology got a big update, notably with the introduction of a screen with "dual-view" technology, which, for example, allowed the passenger to watch a movie while the driver could observe navigation data, and offered the option of creating a Wi-Fi hotspot inside the car. A version of the XJ called Autobiography was also introduced, featuring the best Jaguar had to offer in terms of interior refinement. The engine line-up was revised, too. All were combined with an eight-speed automatic gearbox. The diesel V6 now produced 300bhp and 516lb ft of torque, while the V8 came with a choice of power outputs: 470, 510 or 575bhp. Even the steering system was updated on every XJ: hydraulic power steering was replaced by electric.

XJ

Jaguar's new owner wanted to use the new XJ to introduce a high-end style.

Jaguar XJ (X351), 2010

DISPLACEMENT: V8, 5,000cc; **MAX POWER:** 385bhp; **TORQUE:** 380lb ft; naturally aspirated; rear-wheel drive; six-speed automatic gearbox; **WEIGHT:** 1,755 kg (3,870lb).

C-X75
2010

The film star

At the 2010 Paris Motor Show, on Jaguar's 75th anniversary, the marque lifted the veil on a concept car that was, simply, sublime. The C-X75 was a futuristic coupé, whose pure lines were a landmark in Jaguar's design history. Naturally, the hand of Ian Callum played a big part, but the C-X75 was much more than a mere show car. It was was bursting with technology. In unveiling it, Jaguar was responding to its competitors, including the McLaren P1, Porsche 918 Spyder, Audi R8 e-tron (which was later cancelled) and Mercedes SLS Electric Drive.

Unsurprisingly, Jaguar pulled out all the stops. The C-X75 had a 1.6-litre, four-cylinder engine with a supercharger and turbocharger, but also two electric motors producing 150kW each. Derived from Formula One, the small, 1.6-litre engine had been developed by Williams Advanced Engineering and produced 509bhp at 10,000rpm. This added up to an exceptional hybrid system, with a combined output of 850hp and 738lb ft – the latter available very low down in the range, thanks to the electric motors. Fitted with a seven-speed automatic gearbox (the best there was in 2010), this coupé could reach 100mph in less than 6 seconds, and go on to a top speed of 219mph. The car had been tested at 199mph and, thanks to its deployable aerofoil and underfloor aerodynamics, downforce at that speed was more than 200kg (441lb). In fact, only a Bugatti Veyron could, at the time, rival the C-X75 coupé. But the hybrid also boasted 300kW of electric power, which allowed it to travel 37 miles using only the two electric motors. This supercar also emitted just 89g of CO_2 per kilometre.

At £700,000–£900,000 ($890,000–$1,144,000) apiece, the 250 cars Jaguar planned to produce seemed on the point of finding their buyers. Everything looked ready for a small production run, as had happened with the XJ220 and XJR-15. However, Tata Motors, the marque's new owner, did not want to embark on a game of one-upmanship – at least, not right away. Priority was given to new models that would be produced in much larger numbers. As a result, the C-X75 was never launched.

Nevertheless, in 2015, the C-X75 had one last shot at glory, when it appeared in *Spectre*, the 24th James Bond movie, opposite the Aston Martin DB10 prototype. For the car chase scene in Rome, Jaguar prepared four cars. These stunt-ready C-X75s were fitted with the supercharged 5-litre V8 engine – thereby avoiding putting a much more costly hybrid system through such a severe test.

OPPOSITE

To celebrate Jaguar's 75th anniversary in 2010, the C-X75 made a sensational appearance in *Spectre*, the 2015 James Bond film.

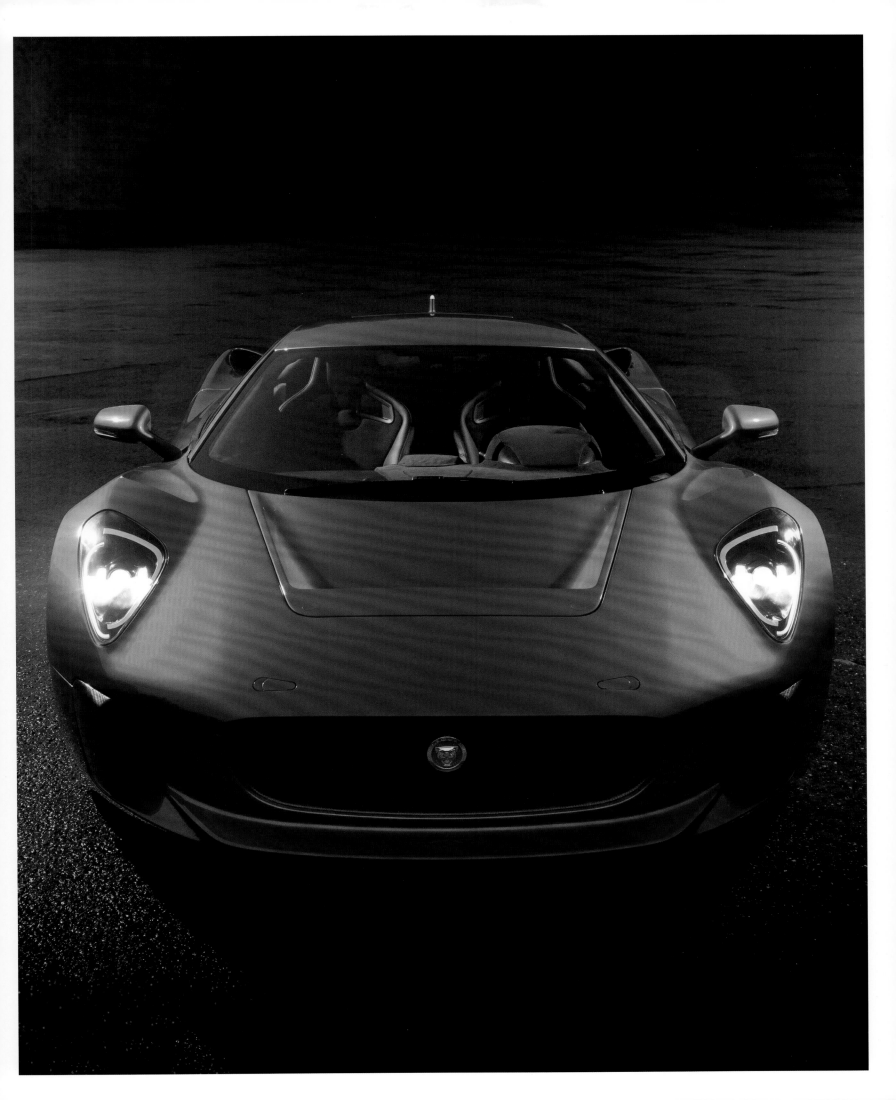

F-Type
2012

Heir to the E-type

OPPOSITE
The proportions of the
F-type coupé were
largely modelled after
the E-type, notably
its heavily slanted rear.

Following the success of the XF, Jaguar had carte blanche to launch high-end sports cars without having to share elements with a mass-market manufacturer, as it had during the Ford era. With Tata, everything was possible. But in 2010, the manufacturer took a big risk, launching a new generation XJ totally different from the XJs that had gone before. Jaguar, which was enjoying the benefits of an almost-new range, wanted to offer a sports car to reconnect with the glorious past. Admittedly, after two generations, the XK coupé and convertible were in need of a well-deserved retirement.

Jaguar unveiled the C-X16 concept car at the 2011 Frankfurt Motor Show. This heralded the replacement for the legendary E-type, production of which had ended in the 1970s. Here was a coupé that was more compact than the XK. It was just 4.47m (14f 8int) long (the Porsche 911 at the time was 4.49m/14ft 9in long), but had quite a long bonnet and very muscular rear wings: the F-type was born.

The production version of the F-type, unveiled the following year at the Paris Motor Show, was almost a true copy of the C-X16 concept car. Jaguar wanted to revive the passion felt for the E-type. So, the striking radiator grille, with the logo at the top, referenced the E-type Series 3. The long bonnet's central bulge, fairly small headlights, minimal rear overhang and

broad wings were details that showed that this two-seater coupé aimed to play the heritage card. Of course, the F-type had aesthetic ambitions of its own – while referencing the past, it also displayed touches that were up to date, even unprecedented. For example, the flush door handles simply emerged when touched, a feature that would also appear later on other models from both Jaguar and Land Rover.

The interior was also upgraded. For a long time, a typical feature of Jaguar cars had been the premium wood veneer on an often-vertical dashboard. But now Jaguar was taking on the Porsche 911, creating a sporty, ergonomic interior. The F-type would also prove Jaguar's ambition, with a range of engines targeted directly at Porsche's 911, but also at the Mercedes-AMG GT.

The F-type came with an eight-speed automatic or a manual gearbox. But the real first was that the F-type, originally rear-wheel drive, was also available in four-wheel drive. Those who liked driving a car with a tendency to oversteer took a dim view of the 4WD option, but Jaguar was aware of this, and gave the car settings that prioritized transmitting power to the rear wheels. The aim was to retain as much as possible in the way of sensation while pushing performance boundaries. Never before had a Jaguar coupé enjoyed such a powerful range of engines.

F-Type

The F-type's long bonnet and rear lights made it the natural successor to the E-type.

OPPOSITE, TOP
Although the F-type's disc brakes were quite large, its side vents were largely cosmetic.

OPPOSITE, BOTTOM
The rear of the F-type, with its elegant rear lights and near-absence of an overhang, was a throwback to the E-type.

ABOVE
The seats of the F-type R were primarily designed to make its occupants as comfortable as possible. This version was especially appreciated on the tracks.

ABOVE
The F-type SVR V8's supercharged engine produced 575bhp thanks to the SVO department. The coupé's top speed was 200mph.

RIGHT
Carbon-ceramic disc brakes borrowed from the competition were installed to stop this 575bhp projectile, which could top 186mph.

At its launch, two models were offered. The F-type S featured a supercharged 3.0-litre V6 with a claimed output of 380bhp – enough to propel it and its two occupants to 62mph in 4.9 seconds, and to a top speed of 171mph. The F-type R was powered by a supercharged 5-litre V8 that produced 550bhp: it went from 0–62mph in a whisker over 4 seconds and had a top speed of 186mph.

F-type Roadster

The roadster version was not long in coming. Like the E-type Roadster, this convertible had a fabric top. But, unlike the E-type, it was stowed away electrically to the rear in 12 seconds – an operation that could be carried out at up to 30mph. Jaguar used a top made up of several layers so that, when it was up, noise was reduced almost to the level of a coupé. The Roadster was available with a "toned-down" variant of the supercharged 5-litre V8, producing 495hp. You could have the wind in your hair up to 185mph…

F-type SVR

The F-type SVR was unveiled at the 2016 Geneva Motor Show. Jaguar Land Rover had just set up the Special Vehicle Operations (SVO) division, and the F-type coupé was the first Jaguar production from its workshops. This version, which had a radically different look, was still powered by the 5-litre V8 engine (AJ133), but its turbocharger pushed the power up to 575bhp. The rest of the car was also upgraded as regards braking system and adjustable suspension, as well as aerodynamics: the active spoiler adjusted itself to the car's speed. The coupé had a top speed of 200mph, the roadster 195mph.

F-Type

In 2016, the F-type SVR launched the new SVO division at Jaguar-Land Rover.

Jaguar F-Type R AWD, 2015

DISPLACEMENT: V8, 5,000cc; **MAX POWER:** 550bhp; **TORQUE:** 502lb ft; supercharged; four-wheel drive; eight-speed automatic gearbox; **WEIGHT:** 1,730 kg (3,814lb).

F-Pace
2015

Jaguar's first SUV

Jaguar unveiled the F-Pace to the press on 15 September 2015, at the Frankfurt Motor Show. Although it was not entirely surprising that the manufacturer, now controlled by Tata, could benefit from all the technology of its cousin, Land Rover, nevertheless the F-Pace marked a historic date for the British big cat: it was the very first SUV bearing the Jaguar name.

The manufacturer had foreshadowed it in the very same place two years earlier, when it unveiled the C-X17, so it was inevitable that Jaguar would take the SUV plunge. Since the market was growing strongly, the company could not afford to miss out, despite its links with a specialist in the field. It must be said that when Jaguar decides to embark on the production of a different kind of car, it creates a stir. The last time it had done so was in 2004, with the X-type Estate.

However, whereas Land Rover's goal was to build 4x4s that were truly capable off road, Jaguar was aiming at customers who were more attached to tarmac. The F-Pace was a demonstration of this, its overall style more dynamic than adventurous. At the front, there was the inevitable radiator grille,

which had also appeared on the recently launched XE. The car's profile had a downward swoop, which reinforced the impression of dynamism.

This Jaguar SUV's mission was obvious: to go after the Porsche Macan on the world's roads. Though almost aggressive on the outside, inside the F-Pace showed much more restraint, with a classic, refined feel. It was as if the manufacturer had intended to shock with the car's look, while reassuring future customers once they were on board that they were well and truly sitting in a Jaguar – an SUV, for sure, but an impeccably elegant one. More unusually, the large screen and instrumentation were also digital. Quite spacious, the F-Pace offered more room for a young family than most of Jaguar's saloons.

All this did not prevent the F-Pace from laying claim to a certain sportiness, as the engines offered demonstrated. There was the now fashionable, supercharged 3-litre V6, producing 340 or 380bhp – perfect for taking on the Macan; the F-Pace, in the S version, boasted 380bhp and could reach 62mph in 5.5 seconds. The engine was matched with the ZF eight-speed gearbox that already featured in other models from the Group. One of the criteria for the

OPPOSITE

Who would have thought? Jaguar joined the high-end SUV market in 2015 with the F-Pace.

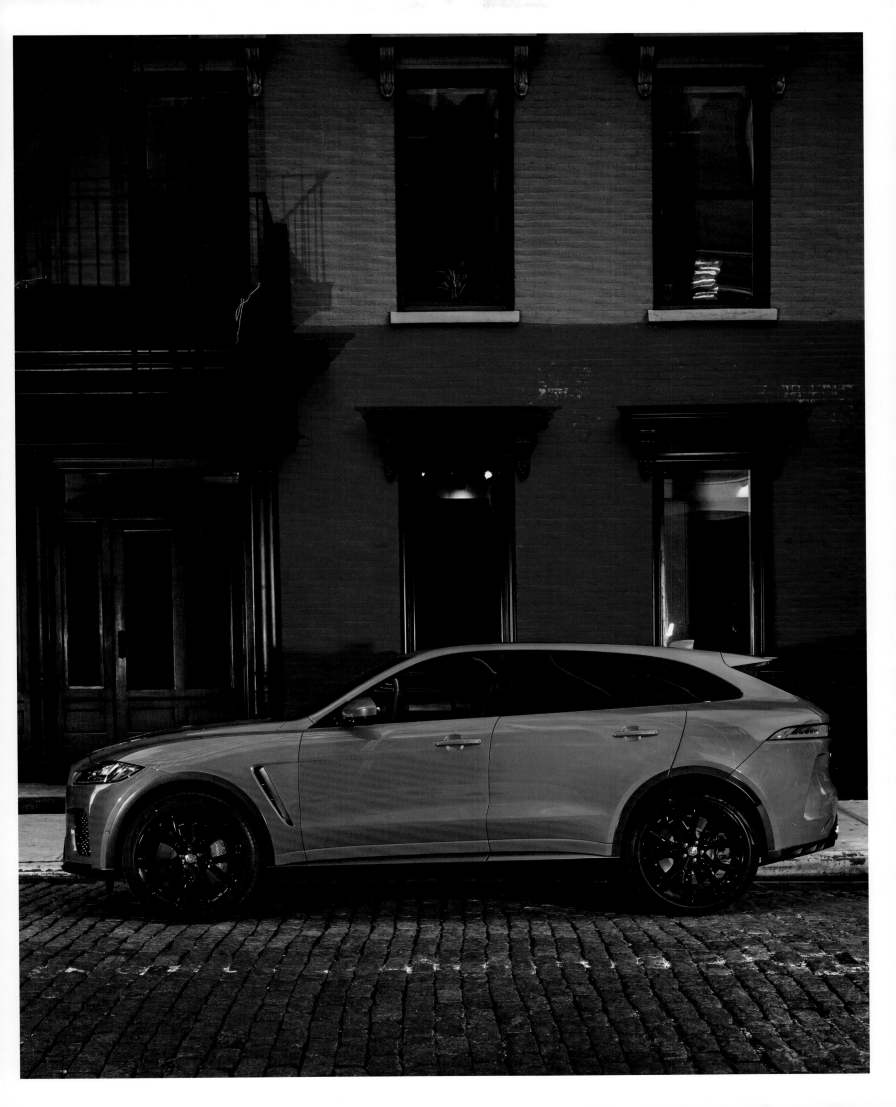

ABOVE
The F-Pace SVR came with a 550bhp V8. It could go from 0–62mph in just 4.4 seconds.

RIGHT
The F-Pace could accommodate the new supercharged 3-litre V6. This allowed the F-Pace S to produce 380bhp and go from 0–62mph in 5.5 seconds.

F-Pace had been that it should be as effective as a sports car. To that end, its suspension avoided excessive roll, making it very nearly as agile as a conventional saloon car. However, that dynamism on the road meant that it had to be content with light off-road use and avoid unduly hazardous terrain – precisely where its Land Rover cousins were able to venture.

With the unveiling of the F-Pace's SVR version at the New York Motor Show in 2018, Jaguar raised its game a notch – it featured the supercharged 5-litre V8, which produced 550bhp and 502lb ft of torque. A real monster of the road, it could propel a young family to 62mph in just 4.4 seconds. It did not offer the comfort of an XJ, for its suspension was generously reinforced. But a family SUV that can hit a top speed of 176mph is still fairly rare these days.

F-Pace

The F-Pace was the first SUV in the history of Jaguar.

Jaguar F-Pace S, 2015

DISPLACEMENT: V6, 2,995cc; **MAX POWER:** 380bhp; **TORQUE:** 332lb ft; supercharged; four-wheel drive; eight-speed automatic gearbox; **WEIGHT:** 1,861kg (4,103lb).

XE
2015

Rich in technology

By 2015, Jaguar was no longer competing with the Audi A4, BMW 3 Series and Mercedes C-Class. The X-type, which had ceased production in 2009, had never been a truly convincing car. Although at its launch in 2001 Jaguar aimed to produce 100,000 X-types per year, at its peak in 2003 it sold around 50,000. The company needed to act quickly in order to offer a younger sister to the XF and XJ.

Even though the F-Pace SUV had already come onto the market, and the E-Pace, a more compact SUV, was in the pipeline, Jaguar needed to re-enter the market for family saloons – notably in China, where this type of car was highly sought-after. Logically, the name XE was used, in order to position this saloon more clearly in the company's range.

From a technical point of view, the XE, which was first unveiled at the 2014 Paris Motor Show, was innovative, with a body that was 75 per cent aluminium and tipped the scales at a whisker over 250kg (551lb). The body structure was also new, and enabled the XE to be stiffer than its bigger

sister, the XF. This modular platform, which would also be used for other Jaguar vehicles, was built in the new Solihull factory. Another important point was that the drag coefficient had been reduced to 0.26, chiefly as a result of the saloon's design. The XE echoed many of the visual cues of the XF and, like the XF, its profile tended toward that of a four-door coupé. It had very elegant lines and, like the F-type, with which it shared many features, was one of the most beautiful saloons launched that year.

Anyone who knew the Jaguar marque well would have noticed a great improvement in the look of the interior and in the materials chosen, especially when compared to its predecessor the X-type, which contained many elements from its direct cousin, the Ford Mondeo. Since the XE saloon did not, for the moment, have a direct link to any of the Group's other cars, the entire passenger compartment was completely new. Although it did not make extensive use of premium materials, a big step forward had been made with regard to information and entertainment, with a colour touch-screen giving faster access to a whole

XE

The interior of the XE celebrated the concept of infotainment.

OPPOSITE, TOP

The high-definition LCD screen was among the XE saloon's finest qualities. Notably, it allowed access to climate control settings.

OPPOSITE, BOTTOM

The XE saloon was a family car whose back seat catered nicely to its three passengers.

ABOVE

The interior of the XE felt opulent. It dropped the high-quality wood veneer in favour of a more high-tech experience, all while providing a high level of comfort.

ABOVE
With a shape worthy of a four-door coupé, the XE series fully embodied the spirit of its two older sisters, the XF and XJ.

RIGHT
The XE's light features were unique, especially its rear lights.

range of functions. The front seats, which could be adjusted in 14 different directions, offered a level of comfort that was exceptional for this class of car. Here, Jaguar enthusiasts could rediscover the expertise of the manufacturer. Headroom in the back, though, was slightly restricted because of the car's profile, with its markedly sloping roof in the style of a coupé.

The engines offered on the XE were essentially four-cylinder, 2-litre units, turbocharged or with a twin turbocharger (diesels 163–180bhp, and the petrol versions 200–300bhp) and a supercharged 3-litre producing 340bhp or 380bhp. Depending on the engine, the XE was available either with rear-wheel or four-wheel drive.

2019: a major update

At the 2019 Geneva Motor Show, Jaguar unveiled an extensive restyling of the XE. For some time, sales had not been consistently good, especially in the Chinese market. Outwardly, this version of the XE did not change much – the main differences were a new, wider radiator grille and headlamps that were 100 per cent LED. The interior was upgraded, with more premium materials and several screens, notably for the dashboard, which could be personalized. The central console had also been modernized. The automatic transmission gear selector was replaced by a more conventional lever fitted with a trigger. The engine range was simplified, with a 2-litre diesel producing 180bhp and two four-cylinder, 2-litre petrol engines producing 250 and 300bhp.

XE

The XE was the only saloon of its class to be made of 75% aluminium.

Jaguar XE, 2015

DISPLACEMENT: inline four-cylinder, 1,997cc; **MAX POWER:** 200bhp; **TORQUE:** 207lb ft; turbocharged; rear-wheel drive; eight-speed automatic gearbox; **WEIGHT:** 1,611 kg (3,552lb).

SVO
Special Vehicle Operations
2015

A new facility

Jaguar needed to respond to competition from AMG (Mercedes), Audi's RS range and BMW Motorsport. These manufacturers, who for a long time had been developing and broadening their sports car ranges, sometimes to include highly radical models, had won a following in many countries. In addition to giving the manufacturers a presence in motor sport, these cars also enabled them to project a strong image, make people dream and appeal to the widest possible audience.

In 2015, Jaguar Land Rover (JLR) launched the Special Vehicle Operations (SVO) division, investing £20m ($25.4m) and employing 100 people in a completely new facility at Ryton, Coventry. The location was ideal, because it was none other than where Peugeot had produced its 206 model until it closed in mid-2007. JLR wanted an exceptional facility – McLaren's site in Woking, Surrey, was to some extent the inspiration – where only extraordinary sports cars were made and where customers could be welcomed like VIPs.

The person in charge was Paul Newsome, who had enough experience of working at Williams Advanced Engineering to react quickly to changes in the market and technological advances. A few months earlier, the manufacturer had revealed the F-type Project 7 at Goodwood, West Sussex, and at the Pebble Beach Concours d'Elégance in California. It met with great success and offered excellent potential for starting the SVO adventure.

In designing this speedster, which was based on the F-type platform, the designer Ian Callum drew inspiration from the D-type of the 1950s. This could be seen in the car's roll cage, the "aero haunch" behind the driver and the short windscreen. Aside from its external features, this F-type was 80kg (176lb) lighter than a standard R version. Its supercharged V8 engine produced 575bhp, or 25bhp more than the F-type R. This gave lightning acceleration – the car reached 62mph in just 3.9 seconds. Jaguar built 250 worldwide, ending production in 2016. All JLR's SVR models in subsequent years would come out of SVO.

But the culmination – to date – for SVO was unquestionably the arrival of the XE SV Project 8. To give an idea, one needs to imagine an XE saloon in brutal mode. The engineers at SVO wanted to combine JLR's biggest engine with Jaguar's most

OPPOSITE
Originally launched under the Land Rover brand, the Special Vehicles Operations (SVO) department also made very innovative Jaguars.

ABOVE
The F-type Project 7 stood for true performance while also paying tribute to the 1950s D-type.

RIGHT
Although the bucket seats of the F-type Project 7 were sporty, they remained very high end.

agile saloon: the XE. At first glance, it was immediately obvious that this saloon was intended to be more than just a modified version of the original. Its front end was meaner-looking than ever, with its carbon-fibre rocker panels, its almost frightening radiator grille and its front splitter that was riddled with holes to cool the big carbon-ceramic brake discs.

This over-the-top XE was even more striking at the rear. The wings were 5.6cm (2¼in) wider on each side, necessary to accommodate the enormous Michelin Pilot Sport Cup wheels, which were more than 30cm (11¾in) wide. To top it off, a very impressive rear wing was mounted over the boot,

to generate the downforce needed by a very high-speed rear drivetrain, for high speed was what this totally exclusive model was about. The "big" engine was none other than the supercharged 5-litre V8, which the engine designers had managed to uprate to 600bhp – enough to propel its occupants to 62mph in 3.7 seconds, and on to a top speed of 199mph. Adjustable suspension made it possible to alter the ride height to suit the driving style, whether on the road or on the track. In fact, it was on the Nürburgring's famous Nordschleife where this family supercar was mostly developed. Only 250 were built.

Special Vehicle Operations

With 600bhp, the XE SV Project 8 was the most powerful saloon of its class.

Jaguar XE SV Project 8, 2018 — **DISPLACEMENT:** V8, 5,000cc; **MAX POWER:** 600bhp; **TORQUE:** 516lb ft; supercharged; four-wheel drive; eight-speed automatic gearbox; **WEIGHT:** 1,820kg (4,012lb).

F-Type rally car

2018

Built for special stages

OPPOSITE
Seventy years before, the XK120 used a six-cylinder engine. Now, the F-type rally car was using a four-cylinder turbo engine. In addition to performance-tuned suspensions and a reinforced chassis, it also contained a rollbar.

In 2018, Jaguar celebrated the 70th anniversary of the legendary XK120 with a rally version of the F-type roadster. It should be remembered that the XK120 had distinguished itself during the 1950s, winning the Tulip Rally in the Netherlands, and finishing first at the RAC Rally – today the Wales Rally GB – with driver Ian Ernest Appleyard at the wheel.

The F-type rally car, of which two were built, had all the features demanded by the FIA (Fédération Internationale de l'Automobile). It was distinctive because it was a roadster version of the F-type, not a coupé, because the manufacturer wanted it to be as close as possible to the XK120 rally car of the 1950s. Externally, it stood out for its banks of four round long-range headlights.

Contrary to what might be supposed, the engine was a 2-litre four-cylinder unit, in order to reduce the weight of the front of the car. Nevertheless, it attained a maximum power output of 300bhp. The rest of the car was totally adapted for extreme conditions: bucket seats designed for racing and fitted with six-point harnesses, a hydraulically operated handbrake, rally-specific tyres and a limited-slip differential were all part of the specification. Although these two F-type rally cars distinguished themselves at the Walters Arena rally in Wales, they were not destined to take part in official special stages. It was just a matter of arousing visitors' desire for the car at the numerous events organized by Jaguar.

E-Pace
2018

The F-Pace's little brother

In 2018, the market for compact SUVs was booming as never before, and sometimes at the expense of large SUVs. This was especially true in Europe, where there was a preference for a more compact, but much more comprehensively equipped, vehicle. Even though Land Rover's Range Rover Evoque was still turning heads, Jaguar launched its first compact SUV – the E-Pace – using the same platform.

In terms of style, the E-Pace was clearly the F-Pace's little brother. At just 4.4m (14½ft) long, it flaunted a particularly sporty look. Compared to its competitors, its very svelte profile and rounded lines made it one of the most elegant and visually pleasing compact SUVs on the market.

In detail, the E-Pace stood out thanks to its radiator grille and slender headlights. The model even took the liberty of echoing the very broad wings and front and rear lights of the F-type coupé!

The interior was also completely new, and aimed at those who wanted to be connected all the time.

This was evident from the fairly wide central touch-screen and, especially, the dashboard, where conventional dials had given way to an entirely digital system. Talking of digital, the E-Pace also featured a 4G connection that allowed up to eight mobile devices to be connected. Jaguar offered a smartphone app, too, which enabled certain settings, such as the interior temperature, to be adjusted remotely.

Although the E-Pace was lower down in the range than its bigger brother, its interior was intended to be extremely inviting, especially with regard to the rear seats, but the boot was also extremely generous at 577 litres (20½cu ft).

Under the bonnet, like its Land Rover cousin the Evoque, the E-Pace was available only with four-cylinder engines, either rear-wheel or four-wheel drive, and a ZF nine-speed automatic gearbox. The turbocharged 2-litre petrol engine was available with a power output of 200, 250 or 300bhp. In the

ABOVE
The E-Pace had a svelte profile with rounded lines, and had a very generous boot.

RIGHT
The E-Pace could be safely classified as a "leisure" vehicle due to its hardy interior materials and a rather high-tech central console.

latter version, the sportiest, the E-Pace could reach 62mph in 6.4 seconds.

It was the diesel version of the E-Pace that sold most in Europe. This, too, had a 2-litre, turbocharged, four-cylinder engine that produced 150, 180 or 240bhp. What this car had to fight against was its own weight: 1.9 tonnes for the D240 version, whereas its competitors weighed up to 200kg (441lb) less. In order to meet the demands of a fairly sporty driving style, the British big cat featured many electronic driving aids, but also rather stiff suspension. Under certain conditions the suspension proved too stiff for some, who criticized it for lack of comfort. The fact remains that the E-Pace was a real pleasure to drive on twisty roads, and a worthy rival to its German competitors. What's more, it had all Land Rover's know-how on its side when it came to leaving the tarmac behind…

E-Pace

The Jaguar E-Pace had the sportiest look of all the compact SUVs on the market.

Jaguar E-Pace P300 AWD S, 2018

DISPLACEMENT: inline four-cylinder, 1,998cc; **MAX POWER:** 300bhp; **TORQUE:** 295lb ft; turbocharged; four-wheel drive; nine-speed automatic gearbox; **WEIGHT:** 1,894kg (4,178lb).

I-Pace
2018

The first all-electric Jaguar

OPPOSITE
The I-Pace Jaguar single-handedly revolutionized the brand. Not only was it the first electric Jaguar, but also the first 100 per cent electric compact SUV.

Although the E-Pace and F-Pace had been part of the landscape for some years, Jaguar did not want to leave it at that for its SUV range. The contribution of its cousin Land Rover enabled Jaguar to avoid spending too much on research and development, but as a new competitor on the market it needed to be innovative. And so the big cat looked to launch itself into spheres where there was as yet very little competition: electric vehicles. The I-Pace was the result. This compact SUV was 100 per cent electric and went on sale in 2018, just after the Tesla X and just before the Audi e-Tron.

Although it was 4.68m (15¼ft) long, the Jaguar I-Pace was still smaller than its competitors, and therefore able to meet the needs of more drivers, notably in Europe where city parking spaces were becoming a rare commodity. In its design, the I-Pace diverged from the rest of the range, with a shape that brought to mind an imposing, tall, compact saloon, with very short overhangs. However, certain details were unmistakable. The front headlights and rear lights – and, of course, the imposing radiator grille – well and truly belonged to the Jaguar family, and directly echoed those of the F-Pace and the XE saloon. The car's sides were concave, like those of a sports car – which is what this (albeit electric) SUV sought to imitate. The aim was to offer a vehicle that was seductive and consumed the minimum energy, thanks to perfect aerodynamics.

The interior of the I-Pace was meant to be more sporty and high-tech than truly luxurious. Like the few electric cars that were launched during 2018, this SUV's enemy was weight. It was therefore logical that its passenger compartment should be a little more minimalist than a traditional Jaguar's. This did not prevent the car from having both a classic and futuristic look, with its numerous screens. Despite the bulky batteries under the floor, this

ABOVE
Unlike most SUVs, the Jaguar I-Pace was able to maintain its sporty appearance despite looking like a lifted compact saloon.

RIGHT
With its 400hp, the I-Pace could reach 62mph in 4.8 seconds without producing harmful emissions.

SUV could accommodate a young family and its luggage, with a generous boot offering 477–1,453 litres (16¾–51¼cu ft).

To power the I-Pace, Jaguar opted for two electric motors with a combined output of 400bhp and over 500lb ft of torque, which meant that this permanent four-wheel drive could leap to 62mph in 4.8 seconds while emitting a sound worthy of a spacecraft. Although one might like the yowling of an F-type's V6 or V8, it must be admitted that the sound is somewhat disconcerting coming from an electric car. But that was the only real flaw in this very first electric big cat. Even with its 2-tonne weight, this small family 4x4 proved to be very enjoyable to drive on all types of road.

What everyone wanted to know at the car's launch was what its range would be. It should be remembered that, just a few years ago, it was rare for an electric car to go beyond 155 miles. Although Jaguar claimed a range of 300 miles, it was more reasonable to reckon on 240 miles – a figure that, even today, is still entirely respectable. Would this be enough to persuade Jaguar to go with the all-electric trend? Very probably.

I-Pace

The I-Pace was the first off-road capable e-vehicle.

Jaguar I-Pace, 2018
MOTOR: electric; **MAX POWER:** 400bhp; **TORQUE:** 513lb ft; four-wheel drive; one-speed automatic gearbox; **WEIGHT:** 2,133kg (4,702lb).

E-Type Zero

2020

Back to the future

OPPOSITE
The E-type Zero electric
engine could reach
60mph in 5.5 seconds
and run for 170 miles.

Almost three billion people worldwide saw the E-type Zero live on their TV screens when Prince Harry and Meghan Markle married in 2018. Jaguar had provided the couple with a new kind of E-type that retained the magnificent shape of the E-type roadster, but its interior had been totally modernized, with screens replacing the small round dials. In spite of the changes, though, the passenger compartment was still extremely elegant and made use of quality materials.

What was most striking about this new E-type was that the six-cylinder engine had been dropped in favour of a 100 per cent electric unit. Located under the bonnet, just like its predecessor's, the motor pumped out 220kW, powered by a battery pack. A minor feat was that the E-type Zero was 46kg (101lb) lighter than the E-type of the late 1960s. With normal charging, the batteries could be recharged in about seven hours and have a range of about 170 miles. Jaguar claimed its performance was on a par with the original car: 0–60mph took 5.5 seconds – that is, one second less than the Series 1 E-type. Tim Hannig, Director of Jaguar Land Rover Classic, explained the design process: "In order to seamlessly combine the new electric powertrain of E-type Zero with the dynamic set-up of the original E-type specification we have limited the vehicle's power output. We believe this provides the optimum driving experience."

The second 100 per cent electric vehicle in the history of Jaguar, the E-type Zero was still at the stage of a working concept car. Nevertheless, the manufacturer gave the green light for small-scale production, starting in 2020. This required the complete restoration or reconstruction of an E-type – which, even today, is a meticulous work of art.

The authors would like to thank the marketing department of Jaguar France, and the marque's press officer, Sandra Bardinon, for their help.

Anthony Beltoise, a talented and passionate racing driver, true connoisseur of the history of the motorcar, and the author of the preface of this book.

Karam Ram, the highly cultivated archivist of the Jaguar Heritage Trust Archive at the British Motor Museum. We would like to thank him for being so responsive and available.

The workshop of JJR Automobiles in Saint-Ouen, near Paris, for their invaluable advice and good humour.

Their families, for their understanding, their calmness, and their tolerance.

———————

PHOTOGRAPHY CREDITS

Preface: Anthony Beltoise DR
Foreword: Jaguar Heritage Trust Archive
Jaguar Heritage Trust Archive: 6, 8, 9, 10, 11, 12, 13, 14, 15, 16, 17, 20 (a), 22, 23 (a), 25, 27, 38, 42, 54, 55, 59, 61 (bl, br), 63 (ar), 66, 68 (b), 69, 73, 85, 99.
Jaguar Press Media: 36, 45, 47, 49, 57, 68 (a), 70, 80 (b), 81, 90, 92, 93, 96, 101, 103, 117, 118, 119, 121 (bl, br), 122, 133, 134, 135, 136, 137, 139, 140, 141, 142, 143, 144, 149 (a), 150, 151, 154, 160, 163, 165, 167, 168, 169, 170, 171, 172, 174, 175, 176, 179, 181, 182, 183, 185–240.
F&L: 19, 20 (b), 21, 29, 30 (b), 31, 32 (b), 34, 43, 48, 51, 52, 53, 67, 74, 75, 83, 87, 88, 89, 98, 106, 109, 111, 112, 114, 116, 130, 155, 157, 159, 161.
Wheelsage: 77, 79, 80, 94, 95, 104, 105, 108, 110, 123 (ar), 125, 126, 127, 128, 129.
Mirror: 120, 121 (a), 123 (al), 148, 149 (bl).
Classic Youngtimers: 147.
Endpapers: Jaguar Press Media
The publisher acknowledges that certain words, model names and designations mentioned in this book are the property of the trademark holder. We use them only for identification purposes.

———————

Jaguar
Text by: Zef Enault, Nicolas Heidet
Originally published by Editions E/P/A – Hachette Livre, 2019

An Hachette UK Company
www.hachette.co.uk

First published in Great Britain in 2019 by Mitchell Beazley, an imprint of Octopus Publishing Group Ltd
Carmelite House, 50 Victoria Embankment
London EC4Y 0DZ
www.octopusbooks.co.uk

Copyright © Editions E/P/A – Hachette Livre 2019
English translation copyright © Octopus Publishing Group 2019

Distributed in the US by Hachette Book Group
1290 Avenue of the Americas, 4th and 5th Floors
New York, NY 10104

Distributed in Canada by Canadian Manda Group
664 Annette St.
Toronto, Ontario, Canada M6S 2C8

All rights reserved. No part of this work may be reproduced or utilized in any form or by any means, electronic or mechanical, including photocopying, recording or by any information storage and retrieval system, without the prior written permission of the publisher.

ISBN 978-1-78472-617-1

A CIP catalogue record for this book is available from the British Library.

Printed and bound in China
10 9 8 7 6 5 4 3 2 1

For this edition:
Senior Commissioning Editor: Joe Cottington
Editor: Ella Parsons
Designer: Jack Storey
Senior Production Controller: Allison Gonsalves

Translators: Simon Jones and Elettra Pauletto
Technical Editor: John Simister

US dollar prices have been converted from sterling using the sterling-dollar conversion rate of 1–1.27, which was correct at the time of printing.